THE HEALING TEAM

A Practical Guide for Effective Ministry

**by
Leo Thomas, O.P.**

PAULIST PRESS
New York / Mahwah

Library of Congress Cataloging-in-Publication Data;

Thomas, Leo, 1922–
    The healing team.

    1. Spiritual healing,   2. Church work with the sick.
I. Title.
BT732.5.T47   1987   259′.4   87-13452
ISBN 0-8091-2909-4 (pbk.)

Published by Paulist Press
997 Macarthur Boulevard
Mahwah, N.J. 07430

Printed and bound in the United States of America

Contents

Section Four:
Ministries That Often Go Unrecognized

Section Five:
Spiritual Resources For Ministers Of Prayer

Section Six:
The Minister of Healing

Preface

This book grows out of my experience of nearly thirty years of training both clergy and laity—Catholic and Protestant—to do pastoral ministry, and of my own priestly ministry to the needs of hurting Christians. For the past ten years I have been on the staff of The Institute for Christian Ministries, based in Tacoma, Washington, which offers a two year training program entitled "Formation for Healing Ministry." Much of what I say in this book comes from this program: some comes from my own experience as practitioner and trainer in the ministry of healing prayer.

My basic thesis is that the ministry of healing prayer does not belong in the category of healing—it is not offering an alternative to the biomedical model of health care; rather this ministry belongs in the category of worship. Its goal is to bring the supplicants into an experience of God meeting them in their needs.

My goal in writing this book is to place this ministry squarely at the heart of the Church's ordinary ministry of pastoral care. That, I believe, is where it belongs because the ministry of healing prayer was central to the commission Christ gave his Church. For this to happen the ministry must be guided and explained by the same theology used for other pastoral ministries, namely by a theology that is incarnational and sacramental. So I have devoted considerable space to explaining such a theology. The writing of this book has also been guided by the conviction that the Holy Spirit, through a revival of the healing ministry, is raising up a large number of people to offer grass-roots pastoral care to fellow Christians. And if the work of the Spirit is to prosper, lay people, as well as clergy, must be trained to do pastoral care informed by the wisdom of the Church regarding pastoral ministry. I have

1

written this book as a practical textbook for those wanting to learn how to minister healing prayer more effectively.

Although I am firmly convinced that God's normative will for us is health, and that the ministry of healing prayer is central to Christ's commission to his Church, I have not developed this thesis. It has been adequately covered by such pioneers as Agnes Sanford, Morton Kelsey, and Francis MacNutt. I presuppose that the reader is acquainted in a general way with their thinking.

The Healing Team should prove useful to all ministers who are interested in learning to use healing prayer as part of the Church's overall pastoral care program—clergy and laity. This would include pastoral visitors to the sick, teams praying on a regular basis with hurting parishioners, and prayer communities that want to develop a sound ministry of healing prayer.

Throughout this book I will use the word "minister" to refer to any ministering person without reference to ordination. Thus, it includes lay as well as ordained persons. I will use the word "supplicant" to indicate the recipient of ministry. My wish is to use language inclusive of both sexes, but I know of no practical way to avoid the troublesome gender pronouns. So I will use "he" and "him" sometimes and "she" and "her" sometimes, both in a generic way for both the minister and the supplicant.

I have taken considerable care to disguise the case materials I have used. So if any of you think that you recognize yourself or another in one of my illustrations it is only because of the commonality of human experiences that we all share.

Original thought is not my gift: mine is to reshape and apply to pastoral practice what I have received from others. After more than thirty years I can no longer remember all from whom I have received. But I do want to acknowledge that I have received much from Agnes Sanford and Francis MacNutt, pioneers in the field of healing prayer; from Thomas Klink of the Menninger Foundation who taught me much about compassionate pastoral care; from fellow staff members of the Institute for Christian Ministries, Dave and Iris Beardemphl, Jim Webster who contributed so much to this book, and the many associates who made our programs possible. Special thanks to Kathy Anderson and Pat King who read the manuscript and made many valuable suggestions.

SECTION ONE

THE HEALING TEAM

1.

Ministry of Prayer for Healing vs. Faith Healing

"Are you a psychic healer?"
"No."
"Are you a faith healer?"
"No, I'm not that either."
"What kind of healer are you?"
"Actually I'm not a healer at all."

The prestigious audience to whom I was speaking looked surprised, but no one was more surprised by that last statement than I was. I was getting ready to show the audience a video tape of myself and three others praying for a mother and her child who had had a traumatic birth. Obviously I needed to explain, perhaps to myself as much as to them, what my ministry in the field of healing actually is.

As a Roman Catholic priest I had many times anointed people with what was popularly called the Last Sacrament. It was a ministry to the dying and the recipient often panicked when the priest arrived with his oil and prayer book; he knew he must be dying or the priest wouldn't be there.

Then the Church drastically changed this official ministry to the sick and gave it a new name, "The Rite of Anointing and Pastoral Care of the Sick." In this revised sacrament we anoint the sick and specifically pray for them to recover. What was so interesting to me was the number of seriously ill people who, after receiving this sacrament, recovered so dramatically.

About that time I found that there were many people, both Catholic and non-Catholic, who were interested and successful in praying for healing. Their ministry was being shaped by numerous books on healing prayer, by the teaching of nationally recognized teachers on the subject, and by various programs of training for the ministry.

As a result ministry to the sick was becoming widely practiced and diversified:

> In a sports arena packed to the rafters a front row displayed a long line of wheelchairs. On the dais a woman in a flowing gown pronounced this one and this one and this one healed of arthritis, ruptured discs or tumors.
>
> In a cluttered living room a man, bald from chemotherapy, lay back on a sofa while four friends knelt around him, read to him from the Bible, anointed him with oil and prayed for his healing.
>
> In a large parish church the priest called for everyone in the congregation who needs healing to come forward for the sacrament of anointing of the sick.
>
> In a downtown hospital a woman received Holy Communion from a lay minister. They held hands and prayed for the woman's healing.
>
> In prayer groups around the country, a hurting person would sit on a chair in the middle of the room while enthusiastic prayer group members gathered around him to pray (sometimes with great vigor) for healing to take place.

I also became aware that the above examples of the renewed practice of ministry to the sick had sparked passionate reactions—favorable and unfavorable. The following are typical:

> Godfrey Diekmann, the editor of *Worship*, a sober and scholarly journal devoted to Christian worship, stated that one of his reasons for boundless optimism in the face of seeming cosmic disaster is the current manifestation of the power of the Holy Spirit which can be seen in the renewed ministry of healing in the Church.[1]

> William Nolen in *A Doctor in Search of a Miracle*, states that he has not seen a single *miraculous* (emphasis added)

cure in following the career of Katherine Kuhlman for several years.[2]

Louis Rose states in the conclusion of his book, *Faith Healing*, that "after nearly twenty years of work I have yet to find one 'miracle cure'; and without that . . . I cannot be convinced of the efficacy of what is commonly termed faith healing."[3]

Francis MacNutt, in his book *The Power to Heal* states that as a result of his ministry about 25% of the people prayed for indicate that they are completely healed physically and about 50% say they are improved, while for about 25% no physical healing seems to happen.[4]

Dennis and Matthew Linn, S.J. in collaboration with Barbara Shlemon, R.N. have written a book titled *To Heal as Jesus Healed*[5] whose main thrust is the power of the sacrament of anointing to effect physical healing as well as emotional and spiritual healing.

James L. Empereur, S.J. in his book *Prophetic Anointing* states: "One can only wonder in what sense physical healing is really an *effect* of this sacrament (anointing of the sick) . . . this sacrament should not be surrounded with the kind of implicit hope or expectation that something miraculous might happen, even if it is only a happy side effect."[6]

These quotes represented the wide variety of opinions regarding the ministry of healing prayer which I was finding existed in the Christian community. Behind this wide diversity of opinion was a lack of agreement about the nature of this ministry. Also I found that many differing theologies lay behind this ministry and that no one had taken the time to examine them. As I began to study and research these differing opinions I made a startling discovery about praying for healing, one that has changed my thinking, even my life. This discovery is the basis for the most important statement I will make in this book. The ministry of prayer for healing does not belong in the category of healing at all, but rather in the *category of worship.*

Let me now explain what I mean. When I was doing library research on this topic I would go to the card catalogue and look under the subject heading of *healing*. Under this large heading there were subheadings such as *medical healing, surgical healing, psychic healing* and *religious or faith healing*. I accepted this way of listing religious healing for a long time and in writing about it found that I thought of my ministry as just one more form of healing—that is, until I was asked to speak to a group of health care workers which included physicians, psychologists and social workers, the group to whom I was speaking at the beginning of this chapter. As I stated, I found myself declining to accept the title not only of *psychic healer* and *faith healer,* but of *healer* itself.

I was not a health care worker. As a minister of healing prayer I was doing something entirely different than they were. I was not one of them. Nor was I offering an alternative to their system of health care as does, for example, Christian Science. When pressed to explain what I was if I was not a healer, I found, again to my own surprise, that after a moment's reflection my answer was that "I am a leader of worship." And that I firmly believe is what the minister of healing prayer is.

What Happens in Worship

Let me tell you a story that will help explain what I mean. Randy was an engineer with the Boeing Company at the time of this story. He came to the sacristy after the Sunday liturgy and said, "Father, something happened to me today at Mass and I just have to tell somebody."

"What happened?" I encouraged him.

He leaned up against the sink and began his story while I changed out of my vestments.

> "For a long time I've been feeling really kind of sick over my daughter, Rosie: just kind of a tight feeling in the pit of my stomach when I think about her. She's twenty and she won't go to college, she won't get anything more than a part-time waitress job, her friends are undesirable and rude and she won't listen to anything I say to her."

He stopped and took a breath and I nodded encouragement to him to continue.

> "But today as I was kneeling there, and I wasn't even thinking about my daughter, I actually heard God speaking to me. He said, 'I want you to trust me with Rosie's life.' And I knew it was God who'd spoken to me and that I could trust him to help Rosie. Right then and there the tight feeling in the pit of my stomach went away."

What happened to Randy was the exact sort of thing that *should* happen in worship. He experienced God's presence and it brought healing. The purpose of worship is to enable a person— or a whole community of persons—to come before God with a need and to experience God meeting that need in the most loving way possible.

In Sunday worship for example, a community comes before the Lord with a need to feed upon the Bread of Life. By the use of sacred space—a special building—by the use of music, singing, color, candles, by the proclamation of God's word, by sharing at the Lord's table, we experience God meeting our need. We are fed; we are strengthened. We go forth with new-found strength to continue walking as disciples of Christ. Baptisms, weddings and funerals are examples of official worship designed to meet more specific needs.

Suffering Fellow Christians

It was becoming increasingly clear to me that the ministry of prayer for healing is meant to enable the person who is hurting— physically, emotionally, spiritually—to experience the Lord meeting her in her need. If the minister uses the many resources at his disposal well, the supplicant (throughout this book I will use the term *supplicant* to designate the person receiving the ministry of prayer for healing) experiences God meeting her in her need.

- She will first of all experience God loving and caring for her.
- Her sense of hopelessness and helplessness will be overcome and she will experience the renewed power of hope.

- She will have experienced the presence of Jesus in the fellowship of believers ministering to her; of believers loving her, valuing her.
- Each one of these effects of worship will affect her powerfully in her total person and healing is to be expected.

The truth that this ministry belongs in the category of worship rather than in that of healing has many practical consequences. The first is that it gives us clarity about who we are and what we are doing. It makes a great difference whether we think that we are health care workers making therapeutic interventions or understand ourselves to be ministers who are enabling a suffering fellow Christian to experience God meeting her in her need.

The health care worker measures the success of the therapy by the degree of improvement of the patient's ailment. The minister of healing prayer measures the success of his ministry not by the degree of improvement of the ailment but by the extent to which the supplicant experiences God meeting her in her need.

Some time ago an article in the news told of a child who had tragically died because after his parents prayed for him they withdrew his medicine, believing that prayer had healed him. Mistaken thinking like this about the ministry of healing prayer, if left uncorrected, will destroy it. The boy's parents thought of themselves as offering an alternative to medical treatment.

We who minister healing prayer are *not* offering an alternative form of treatment; we are not practicing medicine without a license. However, I do want this to be clear: a supplicant *should* expect healing. In the same tone, a doctor should expect that if he does his work well the patient will experience being cared for by God. While both bring healing, the minister and the doctor are doing different things.

A Vulnerable Ministry

Godfrey Diekmann, whom I quoted earlier in this chapter, is right. The power of the Holy Spirit *is* being manifested in the ministry of healing in the Church. People are encountering the transforming power of Jesus in ways we never expected just a few years ago. But the ministry of prayer for healing is a newborn infant, tender and vulnerable. We must learn what we are doing or we can kill it. Both William Nolen and Louis Rose, quoted earlier in this chapter, illustrate this destructive misunderstanding of this ministry with their preoccupation with miracles. Their misunderstanding is common both within and outside of religious circles. They lead people to believe that the ministry of healing prayer is about "miracles."

A good example of this was a woman who had brought her thirteen year old daughter, Tina, to us for healing prayer. For several months, since a fall from a horse, Tina hadn't been able to use her left arm. To our dismay the mother said she had never taken Tina to a doctor. She said, "I just know God's going to heal my daughter through prayer."

At our insistence the mother sought a doctor's help. A simple surgical procedure followed by intensive therapy brought near-normal movement back into Tina's arm. We prayed for Tina through this process and were able to help her overcome the resentment of God that had developed in her heart during the time she had remained unhealed.

"Looking for miracles" means focusing upon an event so sensational that it forces faith from the observer. This fascination with the sensational distressed and sometimes angered Jesus. For example, in Luke 11:29, Jesus says: "How evil are the people of this day! They ask for a miracle, . . . but none will be given them except the miracle of Jonah."

This book is not about "miracles," and the ministry of healing prayer that is described in this book is not interested in performing "miracles." The ministry that this book is advocating must be seen in the context of overall pastoral ministry. When Jesus rehabilitated and commissioned the repentant Simon Peter after the resurrection he did not say: "Work miracles"; rather he said, "Tend my sheep" (Jn 21:16). And when Jesus described himself, he did not say: "I am a miracle worker," but rather he said: "I came that they may have life and have it abundantly. I am the good shepherd: I know my own and my own know me, as the Father knows me and I know the Father; and I lay down my life for the sheep" (Jn 10:10, 14–15).

Real healing takes place in the pastoral healing ministry but it can be measured only in the context of the way the good shepherd cares for his sheep rather than in the context of what a good physician does for his patient. That is why the ministry of prayer for healing is not a substitute for medical treatment but is often a hand-in-hand partner with medicine.

It's my experience that pastoral healing ministry, offered with sensitivity and competence, does produce results. In it I've seen the healing power of Jesus dramatically transforming people's lives. This transformation is manifested physically, emotionally, spiritually and in their relationships. The recipients of the ministry, and those close to them, recognize God's power at work. They experience the care of a loving Father: they know that they have been loved and cared for. They saw that they were being healed in ways they'd never expected.

God Is With Us: He Uses Us

If the ministry of healing prayer is to bear the fruit that God intends, a correct understanding of the incarnation is essential. The incarnation is the model for all of our Christian activity in this world. By the incarnation I mean all that is implied in the text: "The Word became a human being and . . . lived among us" (Jn 1:14). Everything was radically altered once God took on human nature, became a human baby, grew into a child, a teenager, a young man. His humanness has given us a new way of thinking and acting. God chose to reveal himself through created things. This was not a one-time event, but is the model that he uses for all further activity in the world. It is the basis of our use of sacraments and sacramentals. The abundant life which Christ came to bring, now that he is risen and at the right hand of the Father, is continued by the church's use of water, bread and wine, oil, touch, music, in fact through every created being.

This truth has profound implications about how we understand our ministry. I will call this truth an incarnational, or God-with-us, attitude, and I will be returning to it frequently throughout the book. Without the incarnational attitude we would be reduced to merely petitioning God to act. Some ministers, in fact, see petition as the only action on the part of human ministers who are praying for healing. The following illustration will make clear what I mean.

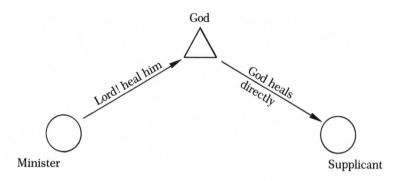

Figure 1

The incarnational attitude, however, sees that God makes use of us to achieve his work. Petition is only one of the ways that we minister healing. God works through us in such a way that the action is totally God's and totally ours. And so the popular slogan "only God heals" is simply not true. The following illustration may illustrate this.

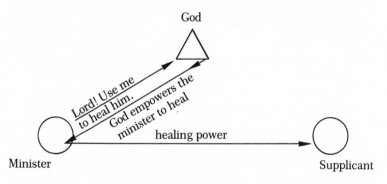

Figure 2

Jesus makes this point when he says in John 20:21: "As the Father sent me, so I send you." Then he breathed on them and said: "Receive the Holy Spirit." We are now the fullness of Christ, that is, the body of Christ. We are the members; he is the head. The task that the Father gave to his Son is being continued in the commission that Christ has given to us. "Jesus called his twelve disciples together and gave them authority to . . . heal every disease and sickness" (Mt 10:1). Through the power of the Holy Spirit God is present to the world through his Church which is composed of all of us who have received the message of Christ in faith.

We have not begun to realize the dignity that is ours: the dignity that carries a very remarkable responsibility. Our eyes are the eyes that God uses to weep for the pain of the world. Our emotions are the emotions that God uses to have compassion upon his people. Our hands are the hands that God uses to bestow his healing blessing upon those in need.

If we do not weep, there are some in the world who will never know that God cares. If we do not lay our hands on others in a gesture of acceptance, there are those who will never experience healing in this world. We have the ability to allow God to use us to build up his kingdom; we also have the freedom to refuse, and so to hinder the coming of his kingdom. This is the mystery of the incarnation: he will establish his presence in the world through the weakness and the limitations of sinful humanity.

My friend Barbara tells this story of how Jesus' love became real to her through the compassion of a neighbor.

"When I was in my late forties my husband died suddenly. For the next two or three weeks a lot of people were coming and going from my house—relatives, my priest, friends and neighbors, a business consultant. There were many things that had to be taken care of. Then everything was quiet. The one daughter still living at home was in school all day. I was alone and wandered around the house feeling numb and lost. I prayed and went to church a lot but I couldn't get my bearings.

"Many times I walked a few blocks to my friend Christy's house. She was young with three small children and I usually found her busy with housework. She would stop and we would go into her homey living room to chat. I would settle in a rocking chair and she would sit on a big round footstool in front of me. Some days I couldn't talk. I would just sit with my head in my hands. She would put her arms around me and hold me. Sometimes she would rock us gently and say things like: 'Jesus, help Barbara feel your deep love for her; to know your heart grieves with her heart; to know you are here.' I only stayed about twenty minutes or so.

"One day as I was walking back home I stopped dead still. It suddenly hit me: that was Jesus! He was using Christy's arms to love and comfort me. No wonder he seemed so close and so real. He was. In her!"

God *is* with us all. In my journey in this area of healing he has taken me on a route I'd never considered years ago. He has shown me that healing happens in the context of worship. When ministered with compassion it will include relational, spiritual, emotional and physical health. The ministers of healing are God's people who are willing to reach out and touch the lives of the hurting people in their world.

NOTES

1. Diekmann, Godfrey, "The Laying On of Hands in Healing," *Liturgy: The Sick and the Dying,* 25:2 (March/April 1980): 7ff.

2. Nolen, William, *Healing: A Doctor in Search of a Miracle,* New York, Random House, 1974.

3. Rose, Louis, *Faith Healing,* Penguin Books, 1971.

4. MacNutt, Francis, *Healing,* Notre Dame, Ave Maria, 1974, p. 28.

5. Shlemon, B.L., Linn, Dennis and Matthew, *To Heal as Jesus Healed,* Notre Dame, Ave Maria, 1978.

6. Empereur, James L., *Prophetic Anointing,* Wilmington, Michael Glazier Inc., 1982.

2.

How To Minister as a Team

Gloria had been a serious dance student since she was a youngster. In order to make the necessary room in her life for lessons and for the demanding hours of practice she had made numerous sacrifices; there had been few leisurely girlhood chats, little free time after school, no pastimes such as skiing or roller skating. As Gloria grew and matured the only thing more important to her than her dancing was her deep and abiding relationship to the Lord.

Prayer, hard work and talent held hands so successfully that Gloria, at twenty, was dancing professionally on the New York stage.

During a dress rehearsal the one thing dancers dread most happened—an injury accident. The injury was to Gloria's knee. A long six weeks went by while she obeyed doctor's orders and stayed off the stage so her knee could heal. But at the end of six weeks the injury wasn't much better. Discouraged that all she had worked and planned for now seemed lost, she returned to her parents' home. That's when she contacted our team and asked for healing prayer.

Four of us, Jim, Dave, Iris and I, met a half hour before Gloria arrived. We gathered in a conference room where we wouldn't be interrupted by the telephone or where our conversation couldn't be overheard. We set a table with a crucifix, a flask of blessed oil, a cup of blessed water, a container of blessed salt and a blessed candle which we would light when we prayed. Iris added a bouquet of flowers. A banner proclaimed that Jesus is Lord. Jim put five chairs in a circle and Dave arranged soft lighting for the room.

With the room readied we chose a leader—this time I was

appointed—and decided on some practical matters such as how
many sessions we could offer and when they would be. Getting
ready had only taken a few minutes; we would spend most of the
half hour in prayer to prepare us to minister to Gloria. Jim played
his guitar and led us in several praise songs. We spent ten minutes praising God in both praise songs and our prayer languages.

Spontaneously we fell silent and I, as the leader, encouraged
all of us to listen to the Lord for any messages he might have for
us. Iris said, "I see an image of a rainbow with God as Father. The
Father is standing behind the rainbow smiling on his children."
Dave softly related, "I'm seeing Jesus walking among us, reaching out and touching each one with his right hand."

I asked Jim to lead us in a song of praise in thanksgiving for
God's encouragement. When we finished, I said, "Dave, will you
anoint us with oil before Gloria arrives?" Using blessed oil he
made the sign of the cross on each of our foreheads and prayed
for special gifts for each one of us that we might minister Christ's
healing.

Before concluding this prayer of preparation time I asked, "Is
anyone burdened in a way that might interfere with the ministry?"

One person raised a hand, "I am."

Someone else prayed immediately, "Lord, please lift this burden. Let each of us be a clear channel of your healing love."

We welcomed Gloria, a willowy, brown-haired young
woman, into our circle and she took a seat between Jim and
Dave. We all knew her so there was no need for introductions.
Since she had experienced prayer ministry before we did not
need to give much explanation. I told her we would be praying
for about an hour.

We held hands and I prayed briefly, "Lord, gather us into one
body. Let your Holy Spirit fall upon us and empower us to minister the healing presence of Jesus that Gloria might be open to
receive any gift that you, Lord, wish to give her."

I asked, "Gloria, in what special way would you like us to
pray?" I already knew she was there for her knee, but I wanted
more detailed information. "Do you think that this injury might
have had harmful effects on other dimensions of your life? Are
you depressed or angry at God because of the accident?"

She shook her head, "No, I felt discouraged at first, but I'm not depressed and I'm not blaming God."

We agreed then to pray only for physical healing. I began, "Let's all of us come into the presence of the Lord and focus especially on the presence of Jesus." Jim led us into five or ten minutes of gentle praise in song and praise prayers. Since Gloria was not comfortable with a charismatic style of praying we did not use our prayer language aloud.

As leader I began praying a prayer of affirmation for Gloria. "Thank you, God, for Gloria's deep faith. Thank you for her trust in your power to heal."

Dave and Iris, who had known her for a long time, both prayed, "Thank you, God, for Gloria's gift of dance. Thank you for her commitment of this gift to your service. Thank you for her love of you, for her self-discipline, for her kindness to others, for her sweet spirit."

After about five minutes of this type of prayer we started to pray in specific and detailed ways for the healing of the injured knee. I knew that Gloria was comfortable with touch, so I suggested that we get up from our chairs so we could gather closely around her. "Let's lay hands on her and hold in mind the image of Jesus reaching out and touching her knee."

Each of us prayed in different ways. Jim prayed, "Lord, bring healing to this member of your body who was injured."

Iris prayed with deep compassion, "Jesus, please restore total healing to my sister's wound."

We spoke directly to Gloria's body and encouraged it to stir up within itself all the healing powers that Jesus had placed there. I prayed, "Body, restore the tissue, cells grow and bring healing, blood bring nourishment to the injured area."

Dave anointed her knee with blessed oil and we all laid hands on her knee and prayed silently in our prayer language. I suggested we sit down and become quiet and see if the Lord had some message for Gloria. Jim strummed on his guitar but we didn't sing.

After some minutes of quiet I asked, "Gloria, what have you been experiencing?"

"I had a feeling of warmth in my knee as you anointed it and laid your hands on it. Also, I have a wonderful conviction that the Lord is healing me."

Dave opened the Scriptures and read a passage he believed the Lord wanted Gloria to hear. It was on how very much God loves her. Again Iris reported, "I see an image of a rainbow. This time one end of the rainbow is actually touching Gloria's knee."

Our scheduled time was coming to an end and I sensed we'd done all we needed to do in this prayer time. I asked the team and Gloria, "Do all of you feel we've finished our ministry?"

"Yes," Iris said, "I feel that this is all we're to do tonight." The others agreed.

"Then let's give thanks to God for what he has done." Together we sang a song of thanks.

Before Gloria left, I asked, "Was something especially helpful tonight?"

She smiled, "Yes, the anointing with oil seemed the most helpful."

"Was anything unhelpful?"

She shook her head no.

We discussed with her the next time we'd meet for prayer and how many sessions would follow. I stood up to indicate that the time of ministry was over and then each of us hugged her and said goodbye.

After Gloria left we remained for a time of debriefing. I started by asking. "How do you think it went tonight?" Jim and Dave and Iris all agreed it had been a good time of ministry.

"Is there something you'd liked to have done differently?"

Dave said, "We could have made more use of the Scripture text by helping Gloria understand more fully what God was saying to her."

We discussed this and then I said to the team, "Let's reflect on those places where God was most evident and where the gifts were especially noticeable." I pointed out to Dave, "Your anointing of Gloria was powerful." To Iris, "There was deep compassion in your prayers of petition." To Jim, "The songs you used were quite appropriate and helpful in furthering this time of healing prayer."

The others discussed how the Lord had guided us in team

prayer. We talked briefly about future meetings with Gloria, sensing that frequent and prolonged prayer was necessary to complete this healing. We gave thanks to God for all he had done and brought our meeting to an end.

Altogether, we met with Gloria six times. Her healing was gradual, but complete. She returned to dancing with no further problem and remains well.

Team Ministry

This detailed example of a prayer team in action should help answer the questions most frequently asked of us, "Why do you minister as a team?" and "What do you do when you pray for healing?"

I strongly recommend that this ministry be offered by a team of two or three people because a team is a more complete representation of the body of Christ, and it is imperative for everyone involved in the ministry—ministers as well as the supplicant—to see that healing flows from the body of Christ. It is Christ the Head making use of some of his members to heal a member of his body.

In Chapter 1 we discussed the incarnational (God-with-us) theology that undergirds this style of ministry. A quick review may be helpful here. Remember the contrasting attitudes mentioned: "Lord! Heal this person!" and "Lord, use us to heal this member of your body." The ministry of healing prayer is more than petition: it is making Jesus present to the supplicant.

The incarnational attitude says that Christ as Head of his body is using us, as a team, to heal a wounded member of his body. A team of two, three, or four people is a more effective channel of Christ's healing power. Several people with their different gifts of personality and talents, as well as their unique virtues and charisms, are better able to make Jesus real to the supplicant.

Another reason to operate as a team is that we draw courage and support from one another. What we might hesitate to attempt alone, we are more willing to attempt in a team.

Also functioning as a team helps to protect the supplicant from the blindness and woundedness of any one individual. The other team members can be a counter-balance to that, can alert us when we are inflicting our woundedness on a supplicant.

Remember, however, that a team is not just a collection of individuals. It is not just any two or three people grouped together for the occasion of this ministry. A team is a body of Christ. It has a life of its own which is animated by the Holy Spirit. Accordingly, this life must be nourished by time spent together in prayer, in reflection upon the team's ministry, in working out relationships, and perhaps in some social time together.

Even though this chapter is concerned with team ministry, clergy, counselors, eucharistic ministers and pastoral visitors to the sick, who find it unfeasible to operate as a team, may be able to adapt what is said here to a solo ministry.

Steps To Be Taken in Praying for Healing

"What does a team do and say to make Jesus real to a supplicant?" This cannot be achieved by following a formula rigidly, but certain ingredients are commonly present when we pray for healing. Sometimes all will be used, sometimes one, sometimes another. I will list them and discuss each one.

Ingredients Used in the
Ministry of Prayer for Healing:

1. **Preparing the Team**
   A. Create a sacred space
   B. Prepare by prayer
   C. Discussion of practical matters

2. **Welcoming the Supplicant**
   A. Introductions
   B. Explain ministry
   C. Brief prayer

3. **Listening**
   A. To the supplicant
   B. To the Lord

1. Preparing the Team

An ingredient frequently overlooked, yet vitally important to the ministry of healing prayer, is the preparatory phase. It is a rare prayer team that has a sacred space to minister in. Usually we meet in such places as classrooms, church basements, and sewing rooms. The story of Gloria illustrates how easy it is to transform an ordinary place into a sacred place.

Don't forget such useful objects as a box of tissues, note pad and pencil.

All of this is merely external preparation. God's presence is what makes the space sacred. In the story of our ministry to Gloria, I indicated how the team came into God's presence by song, praise, use of Scripture and anointing one another. We had already designated who would be the team leader and reviewed what we already knew about the supplicant.

2. Welcoming the Supplicant

After the preparations are completed, the supplicant is invited to join the prayer team. If the supplicant and team members are not acquainted, there needs to be a time of introductions. Names, family status, church affiliation, connections through mutual friends are shared. (The team members should be wearing name tags so the supplicant can learn the names quickly.) This should be brief and take no more than several minutes. There should be no small talk or chattiness, which will *not* put the supplicant at ease. Small talk only confuses the issue of why he is here and makes him more anxious.

If the supplicant has not experienced the ministry of healing prayer, a short explanation of what will happen in this session should be given to him. For example, tell him that there will be a short time of prayer at the beginning, a time when he can explain his need, and then the team will pray for healing.

Tell him how long the session will last. Let the supplicant know how he can participate in the prayer time. Some supplicants are terrified of praying out loud and are relieved to know that they don't have to.

Invite him to ask clarifying questions. Tell him to report what he is experiencing as the team prays for him. Tell him what to do if he needs to stand up for a moment or wants to use the restroom. These details are intended to reduce anxiety by telling him what to expect and to give the supplicant as much control of the situation as possible. The attitude of the team is one of offering hospitality to a weary and wounded traveler on a spiritual journey. Then, before asking the supplicant to explain his need for prayer, it is good to come into the presence of the Lord for a minute or two and seek the guidance of the Holy Spirit. You may also pray that the supplicant may know the presence of Jesus during this time of ministry.

3. Listening

The leader of the prayer team might then ask, "Would you like to tell us what you are seeking ministry for?" The team's task at this point is to facilitate the person telling his story in a way that will in itself be healing. Help him tell his story so that he doesn't get caught in a long monologue of unimportant details or feel alone as he talks, while the team silently looks on.

Some questions may be necessary for clarification or to help the person having difficulty in telling his story. But avoid asking too many questions or it will no longer be his story but merely a question and answer session.

Assure the person you are listening attentively and accepting him as he speaks. This frees the person to express not only facts, but deep feelings which accompany the facts.

As a result of listening, we should be able to say to the supplicant, "This is how it feels to be you," in such a way that the person can say, "Yes! You have understood." To be heard is the beginning of the healing process.

Careful listening will give us the beginnings of an answer to these questions: "Are we the ones to pray?" "Is this the right time to pray? "What should we pray for?"

Listening is not just a phase that can be done once and then left behind. The ministers of prayer must constantly listen, both to the supplicant and to God. There is so much to listen to. The supplicant will frequently give new information; he will report to the team his experience of God working in him as the team prays. The team, too, will experience God giving them guidance as to the direction the ministry should take.

4. Making an Agreement About Ministry

The ministry of healing prayer is not something that is done *to* the supplicant, but rather he is actively involved in the process of deciding upon a plan of action. The plan should include a consideration of when and how long ministry is offered, where it takes place, by whom it is offered, and what hurt will be ministered to. An agreement about these items gives shape to our prayer time. Without them, our ministry is chaotic and disorderly and has very little chance of being effective.

There should be some definite time limits. This is frequently neglected, and such neglect allows the best of ministry to fall into chaos. Both the team and the supplicant should know when they will meet and for how long, and for how many sessions. Prayer for emotional healing will usually require more than one session.

Many people are loath to set a definite length of time for ministry, thinking that they will "just be led by the Spirit" or that it might seem unloving to put some limitations on the time. However, it is quite comforting for both team and supplicant to have some known limits. All of us have other obligations and we must locate our ministry in the context of them. Knowing how long one is going to be in ministry allows both the supplicant and the team to pace themselves. A supplicant can become quite anxious if he does not know how long the prayer team will continue; he is not sure whether he is imposing on the others and he does not know how much to expect from them.

Also, the team will be more effective when it operates within definite time limits. It makes considerable difference in the style of ministering whether it is to be done in five minutes or one hour. For a team working with an adult, forty minutes to an hour is about the right amount of time. It is the team's responsibility to settle on a time to end the ministry. The team, in the initial meeting, or even before the initial meeting, needs to convey to the supplicant that they are willing to meet three, perhaps four, times, after which the team and supplicant will evaluate whether or not more ministry is needed. At the end of the first session it may not yet be known what the root cause of the distress is, but there should be some understanding of the direction the ministry is going.

When the need for prayer has been discerned, and a plan of action has been devised for ministering to that need, it is well for the leader to articulate his understanding of how to proceed. His understanding needs to be confirmed by the team and it needs to be agreeable to the supplicant. For example, the team leader might say, "It seems clear as we listen to you, Gloria, that your only need for prayer is for your injured knee, and since your time is limited, we will pray each day for it for one week. Is this agreeable to you?" We should make sure that the supplicant is in wholehearted agreement with our plan of action. We should never pray for healing of something that the supplicant does not want prayer for.

In this phase of reaching an agreement about ministry, the team can lose sensitivity to the supplicant and sound very impersonal and "problem" oriented. This results in the supplicant feeling that he is a problem to be solved. If the team remembers that in this moment of ministry they are actually being Jesus to the supplicant, their communication will convey Jesus' presence and his loving concern for him.

5. Becoming a Worshiping Community

Having heard the supplicant's need and having reached some agreements about the help to be offered, we need to come into the presence of God as a worshiping community. We can do this a number of ways. We can concentrate our thoughts upon this presence of Jesus. We can praise God with music and song. If someone plays an instrument, this is helpful, but if not, I suggest the use of recorded music and a tape recorder. The use of music lessens our anxieties and puts us in a more meditative frame of mind and makes it easier to concentrate upon the presence of God. Singing is a way of joining together: we are doing something together and in unison. And because most of us are timid about singing, it is a way of "risking" something of ourselves with others.

6. Using the Prayer of Affirmation

I always begin the ministry of healing with the prayer of affirmation—before prayer for the specific need is made. In the case of Gloria, we began by giving praise to God for her great faith in the power of God to heal her. We gave thanks for the gift of dance he had given her, and for her commitment of this gift to his service. The prayer of affirmation will reveal to the person the goodness that God has placed in him, and he will begin to experience the love that God has for him. Love, in itself, is a healing force.

It is not only the supplicant who is touched by the prayer of affirmation. As the ministers pray this prayer, they will find themselves standing in awe of what God has done in this person. They will find their own expectancy increased. They will grow in love and compassion for the supplicant.

7. Praying in Specific Detail

The next step in praying for healing is the prayer of intercession. This should be as specific and concrete as possible. In the case of Gloria, we prayed for the torn tissue to be restored, for cells to grow and the blood to bring nourishment to the injured area. The more you know about the workings of the human person—mind and body—the better you can do this.

8. Praying Imaginatively

I want to emphasize what a powerful resource imaginative prayer is. Our incarnational theology tells us that Christ, our Head, makes use of us to heal a member of his body. But we are not lifeless puppets that he manipulates. He uses us as we really are, fully human persons. God created us in his image. He gave us minds and wills to be used creatively. To create we must have the ability to imagine. The architect must be able to "see" what the house will look like before she can draw up a set of blueprints. The minister of healing prayer must be able to "see" the healed condition of the supplicant before she can pray for it. For the minister of prayer to focus upon the hurt while praying is like the architect sitting at her drawing board and drawing pictures of homeless people and bewailing the fact. But architects do not just draw pretty pictures of dream houses. They have to imagine the processes by which the houses will be built, how the contractor will put in foundations, how the carpenters will build with wood. In the same way, the minister of prayer needs to imagine Christ at work in the healing process. She may imagine him touching or laying on his hands. She may imagine Jesus pouring light into the darkness of the supplicant's life, or activating the natural processes of the human body to destroy cancerous cells.

The team should also instruct the supplicant how to pray imaginatively, both during the time of ministry and in between times. When people are hurting, they frequently need encouragement and support to pray the prayer of faith rather than the prayer of desperation. I have a friend who advocates "praying the solution, not the problem."

9. Laying On of Hands

The laying on of hands contributes a great deal to the effectiveness of the ministry of healing prayer. I remember discussing with a supplicant what had been especially effective in a session of ministry. He said, "The music put me in the presence of God, and your prayers stirred up hope in me, but when you all laid hands on me, I knew you cared." This allowed him to believe that God cared. He attributed the beginning of his healing to this moment.

Make sure the supplicant is comfortable with being touched before using the laying on of hands. Lay them lightly and lovingly on head or shoulders. Remember that you communicate more of your self with touch than you do with words.

There are times when the supplicant will experience warmth or a tingling sensation when hands are laid on, or sometimes the hands of the minister will tremble slightly. These are frequently interpreted as signs of divine power at work, and are many times highly valued by both supplicants and ministers. In my opinion, a gentle touch that conveys love and compassion is a more sure sign of God's presence than trembling hands or tingling warmth. This sense of God's presence may be enhanced by the minister praying imaginatively as hands are laid on. She might pray as follows: "Jesus, as I lay my hands upon your friend, may he know that you are reaching out to touch this hurt, to heal it. Use my hand to convey your love for your friend."

10. Using Sacramentals

Using sacramentals—blessed candles, water, oil or salt— creatively as part of our ministry makes the presence of God and his power to heal more real to the supplicant. I strongly encourage you to use them creatively and to avoid an empty ritualistic use, devoid of meaning. People sometimes ask how to use them, implying that there is *one* correct way and that if they are used in this way there will be some infallible results. This is a wrong way of thinking about sacramentals. The first guiding principle governing their use is to use them in ways that will stir up hope in the supplicant and in the team. The second guiding principle is to administer them with so much love and compassion that the supplicant will experience God's love for him more fully.

The sacramental should be administered with a dignity, and even solemnity, that will enhance its symbolism. The effectiveness of religious symbols is frequently diminished by our careless use of them. For example, anointing with oil from a tiny vial carried in a pocket or purse reduces the impact of this symbol considerably. I advocate a prominent display of the sacramentals in attractive containers to enhance their symbolic value.

Make sure the supplicant understands what sacramentals

are and has a correct understanding of their use. It may be necessary to explain what they are and how to use them in faith. I remember the first time George walked into our prayer room for ministry. The room was dimly lit and a lighted candle was on the table. He looked shocked and asked suspiciously, "What is this, a séance?" If a supplicant does not understand the use of sacramentals he can be quite upset when they are used in ministry to him. However, when explained and used with faith and love, most supplicants appreciate them and report great benefits from their use. It is sometimes a good idea to give the supplicant a sacramental, such as a bottle of oil or holy water or a blessed candle, to take home. Instruct him to use it daily with prayer for a continuation of the healing begun in this time of ministry.

As I bring this discussion of the various ingredients commonly found in team ministry to a close, I want to repeat my opening caution. Your ministry will not always follow the order I have given. You might bless the supplicant with holy water at the very beginning of ministry. You will use song and music and the prayer of affirmation at various times throughout your ministry. I have not given a formula to be followed rigidly, but rather I have been giving elements that must be constructed into a meaningful time of worship in which Christ is experienced meeting the needs of the supplicant.

11. Closing

As the time for ministry comes to an end, certain things should be done. Ask the supplicant what has been especially helpful to him in this ministry, and what has been unhelpful. These questions help him reflect on what God has done, and when and where he has been most present. It gives the team feedback it needs in order to evaluate the effectiveness of its ministry. It also gives clues as to how to minister to this supplicant in the future. Asking what has been unhelpful gives the supplicant a chance to give the team negative feedback that he would otherwise be unwilling to give. Practical arrangements about any future ministry should be reviewed with the supplicant. Then spend a short time of giving thanks to God for the healing process he has begun.

Farewells and leave taking are important, but should not be drawn out. The team leader will have to take charge as most supplicants find it hard to disengage from ministry and will want to socialize. The easiest way to disengage is to be straightforward with the supplicant. Say something like, "We need to listen to the Lord about our ministry and to give thanks to him before we leave, so we need to say goodbye to you now." If the team stands and embraces, or shakes hands with the supplicant, it is easier for him to leave.

After the supplicant leaves, the team needs to debrief. The team leader will help the team review how they functioned as a team. She will affirm each member's ministry and point out instances of God working through each member. She will encourage the team to do this for one another by mentioning some specific gift of ministry, such as a vision, a prayer, or an act of compassion. The emphasis should be on affirmation, not on shortcomings and deficiencies. If there is any future ministry with this supplicant, discuss what direction the ministry should take.

The leader should inquire if any team member is burdened as a result of ministry. If so, the team should pray that he be released.

End the session by saying a short prayer of thanks for continued growth for themselves as a team and pray for any needed gifts.

As you read all of the ingredients needed for effective team ministry, you may feel overwhelmed. You may ask yourself, "How could I ever master all of this?" The process is really not that complicated. I did not invent the various ingredients, but rather identified and named the items that come naturally as a team prays. There is an advantage in identifying and naming what is natural. Having a common language enables the team to talk intelligently about their ministry. Knowing what is involved in healing prayer enables them to consciously give shape to their ministry. As the team reflects upon its ministry, the members help one another to grow in gifts and ability to minister.

Prayer by a team is a valuable resource in ministering to hurting Christians, but it is not an easy ministry; it requires skill developed by training. In the next chapter I will tell the story of one team's experience of learning to minister prayer as a team.

3.

Getting Started may not Be Easy

"Father, our team's in over our heads and we want to quit, but the pastor says we should talk to you before we make our final decision. When can we see you?"

I recognized Jan's voice on the phone. It was subdued and hesitant and it told me that she was upset. Jan was the leader of a newly formed prayer team at St. Mary's Catholic Church. I arranged to see her team the next day. The following story of Jan's team illustrates problems that are common to beginning ministers of healing prayer.

Jan, Sue, and Pete had completed training for team ministry. They wanted to offer ministry once a week in their parish and their pastor had given his full support and had announced it in the parish bulletin. They had already functioned several weeks and had seen several supplicants. This much I knew when Jan called. The following is the story they told me when they came the next day—disguised, of course, to preserve confidentiality.

After Mass one Sunday Larry told Jan that he had back problems. He wondered if prayer might help. Jan gave him an appointment for the coming week. The team expected that praying for Larry's back would be a simple task.

At their first meeting Larry told them that he had been a truck driver and that an accident had severely injured his back several years ago. He was now in constant pain even though he had had good medical treatment including surgery. He had not been able to work since the accident.

His disability caused considerable stress in his marriage and family. They were now on welfare, Larry had large unpaid medical bills, and the bank was threatening foreclosure on their house.

Larry also reported that his sexual relationship with his wife had deteriorated as a result of his injury. He said his wife got tired of his being around the house all the time, especially since she had to care for many of his needs. His children complained that they couldn't have things the way they could before his injury.

Listening to Larry revealed that he was suffering badly from low self-esteem because he could not support his family. His father-in-law blamed him for the lowered standard of living of his daughter and grandchildren. He had said to Larry, "If you were a real man you would get out and work no matter what." This criticism stirred up in Larry memories of his childhood. He had not done well in school and had been criticized severely by teachers and parents. They called him "dumb," "lazy," and "stupid" at various times. He said that as a child he had never been able to measure up to their standards, and now once again he couldn't measure up.

Larry responded to the team's loving listening and told them how fearful he was. He was afraid to do the simplest household task: he might further injure his back and cause even more pain. He was afraid to go out of the house lest he slip and fall. He was so fearful that he could not bring himself to take advantage of a rehabilitation program available to him. This program would help him learn to cope with pain better and then prepare him for a new kind of work.

Larry told them of his anger at the person who had caused the accident. With some embarrassment, he said that he was angry at almost everyone connected with the accident in any way: at the company for whom he had worked; at the insurance company; at the surgeons who had treated him. Encouraged by their acceptance of him, he admitted that he was filled with bitterness and resentment even toward God for "doing this to me."

Although he was not conscious of the fact, the team detected that he probably enjoyed some of the benefits of being incapacitated. He liked being cared for; he liked the leisure to read and to pursue his hobby of shortwave radio. He clearly wanted less pain but it was not clear that he wanted to be completely healed of his injury.

After the team had finished describing the supplicant, I asked them to tell me about their ministry to Larry. Jan said that after Larry finished telling his story the team just sat there in silence feeling completely overwhelmed with his difficult situation. Pete said that it was like being handed the mixed up pieces of three different jigsaw puzzles. I encouraged them to tell me more about their ministry. It took them a while to sort out the details and tell me what happened. In the first session, after Larry had told his story, Sue prayed for his injured back, then Pete prayed for his relationship with his wife, then Jan urged him to forgive all those who had hurt him. They moved quickly from one thing to another until they had covered all the items they could remember. They told him to come back next week.

At the next session, in response to their questions about any improvement, Larry said nothing seemed to have changed. The team was deeply disappointed as they had expected him to report that healing had taken place. They did not know what to do next. They essentially repeated the prayers of the first session. At the end of ministry they were discouraged. In discussion, after Larry departed, the team decided that they should "just turn it over to the Lord": they felt that they had done all they could.

At their third meeting Larry still had no healing to report: his back pain was still intense. The team told him that God always hears prayers; they had prayed in faith for his healing, and now he should "just claim his healing" and not "allow any negative thoughts to enter his mind." They did not schedule any further meetings with Larry. He was polite and thanked them for their trouble, but was obviously disappointed.

In their discussion after Larry left, the team was divided. All were discouraged, but Jan and Pete thought that they probably didn't have a gift of healing, while Sue thought Larry didn't have enough faith. They argued and ended up blaming each other for failing to heal Larry. They felt that they had no future as a team. They told their pastor that they were discontinuing ministry because they didn't think God had really called them to this ministry. That's when their pastor asked them to talk to me before making a final decision because they had been in our training program.

I asked them how I could be of help to them. Jan spoke for the team. "I guess we want your opinion about our decision to end our ministry."

I looked at each discouraged face. "I think it's possible you've reached the wrong conclusion. I think you have some learning to do instead of feeling God has not called you to this ministry." I told them that I would help them with the learning they needed to do.

Initially they were disappointed that I did not agree with them that they ought to stop ministry, but after some discussion they decided to accept my offer of help.

I told them to contact Larry and offer to continue ministry with him, and I would meet with them weekly to help them learn how better to minister to him.

Before they met with Larry I met with the team and reviewed their assets. They had many positive qualities. The team had both sexes; all three had been through the same training; they were ministering under the leadership of their pastor in their own parish. They truly wanted to serve the body of Christ and were not on an ego trip. They were loving and had learned to listen well. (Their ability to listen had encouraged Larry to pour out his story freely.)

I then asked them to pinpoint their problem. They decided that it was not knowing what to do with all the information that Larry had given them. Jan had said earlier that "when Larry finished the team just sat there in silence feeling completely overwhelmed." But it was not only the amount of information that immobilized them, it was also the complexity of Larry's problems. Pete had said that "it was like being handed the mixed up pieces of three different jigsaw puzzles." Each individual had finally responded with prayer but in a haphazard way, and not as a unified team with a plan of action.

The second session with Larry had been no different. The team still had no plan for ministry. Frustrated at the end of the second session they adopted a superspiritual stance in their ministry to Larry ("just turn it over to the Lord"). In the third session, out of this superspiritual stance they put the blame for lack of healing onto Larry ("claim your healing"), and discontinued ministry with him. Blaming each other and deciding to quit their ministry out of a sense of failure were easy solutions for them at that point.

Fortunately their pastor handled this wisely and would not accept their decision to abandon ministry without further discernment. Their abandonment of ministry would have deprived the Church of a valuable resource and jeopardized their own spiritual life by being disobedient to God's call.

What the team needed with Larry was a systematic way of doing their ministry. I asked Pete how he started putting a jigsaw puzzle together. He said that he did the edges first and then an area of one color such as the sky. I told the team that they needed some similar plan and suggested that we review the notion of cycle of ministry—which they had already studied in their training program—as a way of getting started with doing ministry.

Cycle of Ministry

The diagram in Figure 1 shows the sequence of steps or phases of ministry. What I am calling cycle of ministry is really a familiar process that we use in everyday occurrences without being conscious of the fact. I will illustrate its everyday use.

Suppose your child is playing in the back yard with some little friends. You hear screams and cries of distress from your child. You rush out to see what is wrong and you find your child lying on the ground screaming, entangled in her overturned tricycle. The first thing you will do is assess the situation. Are any bones broken? Has she suffered a concussion? Or is she frightened? Or maybe angry? By looking and listening you discover that she was pushed off her tricycle by a playmate and is furiously angry. She has a skinned knee and badly bruised feelings. You have assessed the situation. This is step #1 of the cycle of ministry.

How do you help a child with a slightly skinned knee and badly bruised feelings? Almost certainly a band-aid, probably a chance for her to tell you how angry she is with her playmate, and

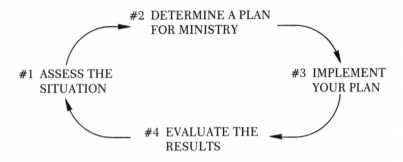

Figure 1

perhaps a glass of milk and a cookie while she has some time alone with you. Out of these possibilities you devise a plan of action. This is step #2 of the cycle of ministry.

And so you take your child into the house, apply the band-aid, hold her while she tells you what she thinks of her playmate, give her several kisses and hugs, and supply her with a cookie and glass of milk. You have implemented your plan. This is step #3 of the cycle of ministry.

You notice that your child has stopped crying, is climbing down from the table and says she wants to go out to play. You conclude that the problem is finished and that you can return to washing the dishes. You have evaluated the results of your ministry. This is step #4 of the cycle of ministry.

But if after the band-aids, cookies and hugs she is still whimpering and clinging on to you, your evaluation would be that something more is needed. The cycle would begin again. You would return to step #1 and reassess the situation. Perhaps she is overtired and cranky. You develop a new plan of action—put her down for a nap—which you implement. If she is her usual self after the nap you evaluate your plan of action as successful and the event is finished.

The cycle of ministry is indeed a natural way of helping others that we use every day. But unless we make it a conscious process, identifying each step and giving them names, we will forget to use it in situations that are complex and bewildering.

Then we become overwhelmed. It might be quite different if upon hearing your child's screams you discover that she has wandered into the street and has been struck by a truck and is bleeding profusely. You might very well panic and not be able to do anything helpful. The paramedic, on the other hand, has been trained to use the cycle of ministry approach even in the face of a trauma and will automatically do so. We need to learn to do likewise in our ministry.

After reviewing the material in a general way with the team, we then applied each phase of the cycle to their work with Larry.

Phase #1: Assessment

In the assessment phase we listen to the supplicant to determine what wounds we will minister to. I asked the team to review what Larry had told them in the first session with these questions in mind: "How has the hurt in the physical dimension affected the other dimensions of his life?" "What is Larry's core problem?" "How open is Larry to receive healing in these other dimensions?" "What are Larry's strengths and weaknesses?"

As the team did this assessment they were able to see that Larry's back injury had indeed affected the other three dimensions of his life. Emotional hurts from his past had been stirred up, his important relationships had suffered as a result of the injury, and his inordinate anger and alienation from God showed that his spiritual life was suffering. But they also thought that the physical injury was not really the cause of these problems, but only the event that brought them to the surface: that even if his back were completely healed the other problems would still be there, though in less severe form. They thought that perhaps the core problem was his damaged self-esteem from receiving so much criticism in his childhood. They decided that they did not know how open Larry was to receive ministry for these other wounds, but that this would have to be tested out by further conversation with him. They recognized two strengths in Larry. His emotional life was basically healthy, and in spite of his present anger toward God, he was a deeply religious man.

I asked the team if they had been listening to God as they

listened to Larry. We sometimes receive information about the person that seems to come from God. People "hear God" in many different ways. Some report that they hear an inner voice: not with their ears but with their mind. For others it is more like a thought occurring to them. For still others, it is more like a hunch that needs to be tested. The team said they were so busy listening to Larry that they didn't remember to listen to God. If they had remembered to do so, God might have revealed a deeper reason why Larry was so angry and blaming so many people for his troubles. In fact without realizing it, the team may have "heard" from God that Larry was ambivalent about receiving complete healing.

I told the team that they had done a good job of making an initial assessment. They had a good idea of the wounds that were preventing Larry from being the person God intended him to be, and some conjectures about the core problem. It is not to be expected that a complete assessment can be made at the end of the first session. It will gradually become clearer as ministry continues. Also, it is usually impossible to come to a common agreement about the problem until the team is alone and can talk and pray about it. So the team needs to depend upon the leader's guidance of the prayer during the remainder of the first session. This prayer can be of a general nature so that it does not commit the team to a permanent course of action. Prayers of affirmation, prayer that God's love will engulf the supplicant, and prayer that the supplicant will experience Christ's healing presence are all valuable ways of praying in this first session, but do not presuppose that a complete assessment has been made.

The team had made its initial assessment of Larry's hurts. It was now time to move into a discussion of a proposed plan of action.

A Plan of Action

Ordinarily the first decision for the team in making a plan of action is whether they are called to minister to this supplicant. In this instance the team had made the decision to continue with Larry because I had recommended it. But even so, I took the team through the process of making this decision. I asked the team to consider such questions as: "Is prayer the proper way to bring healing to Larry's hurts?" "Are we as a team qualified to minister to Larry?" The answer to this will depend upon the kind and severity of the supplicant's woundedness, and the team's talents, training, and experience. Although they were nervous they decided that they could minister to Larry with my support.

A team also needs to ask such questions as: "Do we have the time and energy to give this supplicant the ministry he needs?" "Are we able to respect, love, and have compassion for this supplicant?"

The team responded that prayer did seem to be an appropriate rememdy for Larry's needs as he was receiving medical help. The team was newly formed and was not yet overscheduled, so there was no problem about time and energy. They liked Larry and there was much about him that they respected. The only real question for the team was whether they were qualified to minister to Larry's hurts. His hurts were complex and the team was not very experienced. I led them through a discussion of their talents and training and they decided that if I would continue to meet with them they could minister to him. I agreed to meet with them after each session with Larry for the next three weeks.

If a team decides that it is not the team to minister, considerable delicacy is needed to communicate this to the supplicant and to help him get the ministry he needs.

The next item in formulating a plan of action is to define the need or needs that the team will minister to, and if there is more than one need, in what order to take them. The plan includes what *not* to pray for. A team should not think that it has to pray for every need. Every supplicant will have more needs than any prayer team could possibly meet. For some of these needs the team might make a referral. For example in the case of Larry the team might suggest that he and his wife make use of a marriage counselor.

Making a referral would not mean that the team would not pray in any way for his marriage. The counseling might uncover the need for inner healing of wounds which are disrupting the marriage. Or the team might pray that God would empower the counselor to bring healing to this marriage.

Before entering into ministry the team must have some strategy for their ministry. A team cannot pray for a supplicant's every need. The strategy might be to pray only for the explicit request. But sometimes a more basic wound needs to be healed before the explicit request can be met. Sometimes the strategy will be to pray for a need where there is the greatest likelihood of success. A small success in a significant area of the supplicant's life can have far-reaching effects. It can build the supplicant's faith and overcome her feelings of hopelessness.

I asked the team to formulate a plan of action for Larry in light of their assessment of his difficulties. They decided that in their first meeting they would review with Larry the problems he had already shared with them, and then ask him for which of those would he like ministry. They would only pray for one need in this first session. And they would ask Larry to give them a lot of feedback as they ministered to him. They would encourage this by such statements as: "Tell us what are you experiencing as we pray." "Tell us if you are feeling uncomfortable with what we are doing." "Are you hearing anything that seems to be from God?" They would be prepared to follow up on his feedback.

I made two additions to their plan. The first was that they use the prayer of affirmation at every reasonable opportunity. This would be healing to his damaged self-image. The second was that they make frequent use of peaceful instrumental music, and that during the music they should pray quietly for guidance from the Holy Spirit. They would receive this guidance by paying attention to the thoughts and images that came to them in this prayer time, and by discussing them as a team and with Larry when it seemed appropriate to do so.

I further recommended that they not move to prayer for a new need until they had talked it over with Larry.

My most important recommendation was that they very consciously foster love for Larry. They did not need to express it in words. They should spend a good amount of time praying with images that God's love would envelop Larry.

As we were ending our session, I asked them to be prepared to report in our next meeting what happened as they implemented the plan of action.

Phase #3: Implementing the Plan

Much of what needs to be said about implementing the plan has already been covered in Chapter 2, *How To Minister as a Healing Team,* and some of the resources available to prayer teams will be discussed in the next chapter. But at this point, before reporting what the team did with Larry, I want to discuss some difficulties teams sometimes experience in implementing their plan.

The logic of the cycle of ministry is that you assess the need, devise a plan to meet that need, and then actually carry out that plan. That seems simple and straightforward. But teams do not always carry out the plan of ministry they have devised. Why not? That is what I want to discuss here.

Sometimes a team lacks the skill or knowledge needed to follow out its plan, but the most common reason is getting distracted. As ministry progresses the supplicant reveals new information about himself: new wounds or new reasons accounting for his woundedness. When this happens, the team should return to the assessment phase, reassess the need and revise the plan of action, if necessary, and then implement the revised plan. But what can happen is that the team becomes fascinated with some aspect of this new information. Then, without going through the cycle of ministry, they attempt to minister to this newly discovered need. But before even this new one is healed they get fascinated with still another and so on. I call this "chasing rabbits." It is like a dog on a rabbit chase. Before he catches one, another pops up. He leaves the trail of the first one and starts chasing the new one.

Another reason for not following out the plan of ministry is forgetfulness. This may seem strange but remember that the ministry frequently extends over many weeks. And so the team and even the supplicant can easily forget the original plan. They then gradually drift into a new plan or minister to new needs without even being aware they are doing so. It is the duty of the team leader to keep the plan firmly in mind and not to let the team get distracted or forgetful.

The worst reason for not implementing the plan of action is

lack of commitment on the part of the ministers. When the ministry extends over a long time the team can become weary or bored with the process and just quit. They forget the loving commitment of fidelity they have made to the supplicant. Usually they find some excuse to end ministry prematurely. This is damaging to the supplicant. It reinforces her sense of hopelessness, and is usually experienced as rejection.

The St. Mary's team had never devised an explicit plan of action, but their implicit plan was that a single prayer for every need he mentioned would bring immediate healing. When that did not happen the frustrated team quit the ministry with Larry prematurely.

I met with the team the day after the first session of their renewed ministry to Larry. This time they came with smiles and excitement. They were so eager to report what had happened that I had to ask them to let Jan tell the story and then they could add their perceptions. She said the first thing they did was to discuss with him their premature termination of ministry.

Jan said that Larry had blamed himself for the failure to achieve healing. He had said, "I failed to measure up once again. I decided that I was hopeless and that God had given up on me. I am so glad that you are going to give me another chance." Jan said that Sue had started to cry and asked his forgiveness for ending ministry just when he needed them most. Then Jan had led Larry and the team through a discussion of their feelings about having ended ministry prematurely. It settled the feelings of both Larry and the team and helped them re-establish rapport.

Jan then moved them into implementing the new plan for this first session. They reviewed with Larry the problems he had shared with them as they remembered it and then asked him where he would like to start ministry. To their surprise he said that he thought they should start with inner healing: with the childhood experience of never being able to measure up. He had come to this decision as a result of his discussion with the prayer team at the beginning of the meeting about his feelings of not measuring up to their expectations.

They had started the prayer time with a generous amount of

praise using music and song. They had a deep sense of God's presence. They then used the prayer of affirmation generously. Larry began to sob. In response to their invitation to share what was happening, he told them that he experienced God himself affirming him. For the first time in his life he felt God's approval of him.

The team stayed with this experience for a long time. They prayed, using images, for God's love to envelop Larry. They also spent time silently loving Larry. Peter reported an image of God as Grandfather holding Larry as a child on his lap and rejoicing in him as only a grandparent can do. This led the team to begin praying for healing of his childhood experience of being ridiculed for not "measuring up."

They asked Larry to remember some particularly painful experience of being ridiculed. After a minute Larry began to cry. The scene he remembered was a time when he had brought home a report card with a failing grade in English composition. His father had made him wear a dunce cap at the dinner table and berated him for being the family "dummy." From then on his brothers and sisters would call him Dummy when they wanted to tease him. He would lash out in anger and then get punished by his father for his temper. The team had told him to invite Jesus into this scene. He did so and had a powerful experience of Jesus turning the whole scene around, healing his hurts and bringing reconciliation to the family members.

At the end of the hour both Larry and the team were completely exhausted but joyful. Jan asked Larry, "Was anything we did tonight especially helpful?" Larry nodded, "The most helpful thing was when the team asked me to give them feedback as they ministered to me. I thought to myself, they must think I have something valuable to contribute to this prayer for healing or they wouldn't be asking me for feedback." He said further that this gave him confidence to believe that his experiences of God were real.

Since our conversation was sliding into an evaluation of the team's ministry I suggested that we consciously move into a discussion of the fourth phase of the cycle of ministry.

Evaluation of Ministry

Even while in the midst of actively implementing our plan for ministry we are constantly evaluating it. In the back of our minds we have such questions as: "Is our ministry producing the intended results or not?" "If not, why not?" "Is it doing something we had not intended?" "Is this good or bad?" But at certain points in ministry a more deliberate and conscious evaluation needs to be made. For example, there should be a short time of evaluation at the end of each session of ministry with the supplicant and later by the team alone. A longer period of evaluation with the supplicant is necessary after the scheduled number of sessions have occurred. An evaluation is called for when the goals for ministry set at the beginning seem to have been reached, or when it seems that no progress is being made.

Although he did not use the word "evaluation," this, in fact, is what the pastor of St. Mary's suggested to the team when it wanted to disband. When they came to me the first thing we did was to evaluate their ministry. Through this process they discovered what was lacking in their ministry, decided it could be remedied and so resumed their ministry to Larry. If they had not used this phase of the ministry cycle their ministry would have been lost to the Church.

Evaluation is also the best of all possible ways to learn. It is learning by reflecting upon one's own experience. If it is done frequently enough in planned and formal ways it will become so habitual that our ministry will always be a learning experience. (See Appendix B for guidelines for self-reflection on team ministry.) Evaluation, then, enables us to grow in our ability to be an instrument of God's healing power.

To move the St. Mary's team into a time of explicit evaluation I asked them to rate their ministry to Larry using a scale of 1 to 10. Sue immediately placed it at 10, Pete thought 9, and Jan said 8 or 9. I then took them through a standard check list (see Appendix A) and asked them to note what they had done well and what they had done poorly or forgotten to do. They had been deficient in only a few items. They had been so nervous before meeting Larry that they had not prepared very well. And they had been so excited at the end that they had not given clear instructions to Larry about future meetings. Nor had they done well in debriefing after Larry left. However, I told them that for an inexperienced team they had done unusually well.

I met with the team two more times. After that they felt confident enough to continue ministry to Larry without my help. About a year after our last meeting Jan made an appointment with me to report the outcome of their ministry with Larry. They had met with Larry a total of eight times, not counting the first three before they came to me. About a year after their first meeting Larry asked if he could meet formally with the team on the anniversary of their first meeting to thank God for what he had done. Larry had brought each of them a card with a personal message and a small gift. He thanked them for what they had done for him and his family, and asked if together they could offer a prayer of thanks to God.

Larry enumerated the benefits of their ministry. He said, "When you concentrated on prayer for inner healing my sense of never measuring up gradually subsided." Toward the end of the prayer ministry he and his wife had entered marriage counseling and their relationship was now "just great." Larry had made use of a financial counselor, and had taken advantage of the rehabilitation program available to him. As a result he now had a steady job as an electronics repairman for a computer firm. Larry said, "My back never completely healed but I went to a pain clinic and have learned to handle the pain better. It doesn't bother me much anymore." But Jan reported Larry as saying, "The best thing that happened is my relationship with God. Every day I feel God's love and care for me and my family." Larry's concluding words were, "I'm a changed man: I'm a living miracle."

I asked Jan what she thought had been the most important thing the team had learned through their experience with Larry. She said that in one of their meetings with me I had said, when talking about the cycle of ministry, " 'Trust the process: when you don't know where you are going, follow the cycle of ministry and the steps to be taken in praying for healing' (listed in Chapter 2). In fact we wrote both of them out on small cards for each team member and kept them before us during ministry for a long time." This statement had become a slogan for them. She said, "We would like to have every step made clear to us before we even begin ministry, but we know that is impossible. We have come to believe that God will lead us step by step. And we have to take each step in faith that it will lead to the next step. That is what 'Trust the process' has come to mean for us."

SECTION TWO

CHRISTIAN LISTENING:
A HEALING ART

4.

Listening: A Divine Activity

"Fr. Leo, this course is supposed to teach us how to pray for divine healing and you are teaching us man-made techniques of counseling."

Mildred's troubled voice came from the middle of the classroom. I was standing in front of sixty-five people enrolled in the Formation for Healing Ministry program in Seattle. The main point of my presentation was the need to listen to the supplicant before praying for healing. I had just finished saying that the kind of responses we make will help or hinder the supplicant from telling us his story, when Mildred interrupted.

This was not the first time Mildred had been upset by my teaching. She had been puzzled and disturbed in an earlier class in which I had said that our ministry makes present the person and ministry of Jesus. She had been especially upset when I said that as we act "in Christ" the action is both fully human and fully divine. I felt sympathy for her puzzlement. It is hard to grasp St. Paul's teaching that when we are "in Christ" God uses us, as members of Christ's body, to reconcile the world to himself (2 Cor 5:20–21).

In the silence that followed Mildred's interruption I wondered how I could help her understand her dignity as a Christian. I wanted her to know that her ministry makes Christ present to the suffering supplicant. How could I help her grasp that pastoral listening is a divine activity as well as a human one?

I have learned that experience will teach when words fail—even the experience of role-playing. So I asked Mildred if she would be willing to role play a situation. This would be her "script."

"You are Mary, an unmarried woman of 22, from a small town and now in a big city. You have been working as a sales representative for a famous advertising agency—your first important job. Dan, your boss, has taken a special interest in you. He has helped you learn your way around in the advertising world and in the fast social scene. This relationship has developed into an 'affair.' Dan has made it clear that he is committed to his marriage even though he 'cheats on his wife.' Today a medical examination has confirmed your fear that you are pregnant by Dan. You have told Dan. He is angry and wants you to have an abortion. You are really upset. You don't want an abortion, but don't see any other way out. You don't know where to turn for help. You decide to talk to Jane your roommate. You hope she will have an answer."

Mildred agreed to do the role-play. Irene, who was teaching with me, would play the part of Jane. Jane's "script" described her—Jane—as being very religious, but self-righteous and moralistic. She truly loves Mary but disapproves of her lifestyle and wants Mary to be more religious.

The role-play starts in their shared apartment the evening Mary has found out about her pregnancy.

"How was your day, Jane?"

"O.K. Same old thing. Drudgery at work. I'm glad to be home to relax. How was yours?"

(Deep sigh from Mary. Hesitantly.) "I didn't have a good day. I didn't go to work."

"You didn't! How come?"

"I went to the doctor today."

"What's wrong?"

(Another deep sigh and long pause.) "I'm pregnant!"

(With obvious shock.) "You're what!" (Then in scolding tone) "Mary, I told you that your were playing with fire. And now you've got burnt."

"Don't scold me, Jane. I thought I could count on you. I'm hurting—bad."

"I can see that, and you can count on me. I'm here. I want to help. And I'm listening, but I'm shocked."

(Angrily) "I didn't expect you to be shocked. I'm in a tight spot. I expected you to have some feelings about *me*."

"I do. I really love you. I feel so bad about this . . . (pause) But I guess I thought you were smarter than to get yourself in a mess like this."

(Sarcastically) "You're supposed to be a friend. Forget it. I don't want to talk anymore about it. I really needed someone to talk to. But I guess I'm going to have to go it alone. I'm leaving."

"Where do you think you're going to go? I think you need help. You stay right here and talk to me. What are you going to do about the baby?"

"That's the problem. Dan wants me to have an abortion. If I don't he'll fire me. I don't know what to do. I can't have a baby with no money and no job. And I can't tell my parents. It would kill them."

"I'm ashamed of you for even thinking of murdering your baby. How can you expect God to help you if you commit that sin? I think it's about time that we pray about this. You need to ask God's pardon and then maybe he will give you a way out."

"A big help you are. I'm really hurting. I'm scared and I came to you because you're religious and I thought you would help me. And all you're interested in is saving my soul. I'm leaving." (Angrily gets up and leaves the scene breaking the simulation.)

The Damage Caused by Not Listening Deeply

Following the role-play Mildred said she was amazed at the powerful effect the simulation had upon her. As she read the instructions she became sad and felt tears welling up. As she acted the part of Mary she felt a desperate need to pour her heart out and was hoping Irene would play the role of Jane in loving ways. As she entered the role-play she felt frightened, confused, and cornered. She felt genuine anger at the way her roommate talked to her. Mildred said that she could not believe that she was being treated in such an unloving way. But even so, when Jane made more offers to help she would try again to be heard. Finally she was not willing to talk anymore, let alone pray, with Jane. At the end of the role-play she felt deeply betrayed by her roommate.

This role play illustrates a real-life mistake—both serious and frequent—of praying with a supplicant before listening deeply to his story. The result is that the ministers don't know what God has been doing in the supplicant's life and what areas have not yet been touched by God. And so they pray badly. But even if they are "on target" the supplicant usually does not experience God's presence because he has not yet been heard by God through the team's listening. Christian listening is more than a human skill. When done "in Christ" it is a divine activity, based upon faith and exercised in love.

I noticed that even though the role play was finished Mildred continued to be upset. I mentioned this and she said, "Yes, I am still upset. I know that Irene was just playing a role and following directions in her 'script,' but I am still angry with her. I feel uncared for and can't seem to let go of the role." The class was having similar feelings. So I asked if it would be helpful to repeat the role-play with the listener taking a helpful stance. Mildred and the class thought it would be and Mildred agreed to do the role-play again. I asked Leonard, a staff member, to play the listening stance. His "script" was to play Mary's favorite uncle, Ed, who was a priest. He would listen carefully and be as helpful as possible. But before I report what happened in the new role-play, I want to reflect further on the first one.

Why was Jane not helpful to Mary? After all they did have an established relationship as roommates. Jane did love Mary and did have her welfare at heart. The answer is that Jane failed in the most crucial task of a helper: that of establishing a *healing* relationship. How does one do this?

Qualities of a Healing Relationship

In the early 1960's two psychologists, Traux and Carkhuff, established that three qualities are indispensable for a healing relationship. They are:
1. Accurate empathy
2. Non-possessive warmth
3. Genuineness

Accurate Empathy

Empathy is the ability to know what it feels like to be *this* person in *this* situation. It is the ability to "get into the skin of another." Most people use it naturally in everyday situations but without an awareness of doing so. For example, a kindergartener comes downstairs to breakfast complaining that he is too sick to go to school today. His mother touches his forehead, observes him carefully, listen to his tone of voice and decides there is something more to this than being sick. She responds by saying: "That's too bad. Are you going to miss anything important at school today?"

The child responds: "No, just a dumb old tasting party. We are going to taste pomegranates and artichokes."

The mother responds by saying: "And you hate artichokes don't you? Would it help if I wrote a note to the teacher saying you didn't have to taste artichokes?"

The child responds "Yeah" and indicates that he is now ready to go to kindergarten. The mother accurately understood what it felt like to be *this* child faced with *this* unpleasant situation, and not knowing how to handle it. Empathy is an everyday matter for a parent. Of course, some have it naturally to a greater degree, but it can be learned and developed.

Jane was not able to have empathy for Mary in her situation because she had other plans. She wanted to make Mary understand that her behavior had been wrong and had brought this consequence as a punishment. ("Mary, I told you that you were playing with fire, and now you've got burnt.") Jane also wanted to prevent her from compounding the mistake by having an abortion. ("I'm ashamed of you for even thinking of murdering your baby.") Jane's personal agenda prevented her from feeling how cornered and trapped Mary felt. Mary, because she did not experience being understood, was not open to Jane's solutions.

Non-Possessive Warmth

To be truly helpful we must love the person with *agape* love. This is the kind of love with which God loves us. William Barclay, a renowned Scripture scholar, defines *agape* love as "invincible good will, unconquerable benevolence." God refuses to treat us as an enemy. He loves us even in our sinfulness. He does not make us earn his love.

The psychologists' term, non-possessive warmth, is related to *agape* love. As a Christian minister I will love the supplicant with God's love: I will love her just as she is. She does not need to act or talk in a way to earn my love. I do not love her on condition that she give up her sin. Of course in desiring the very best for her, I hope that she will give up sinful ways, but I do not withhold my love until she does so.

Jane was not able to show this kind of warmth to Mary. Undoubtedly she felt what many people do—that if she was "soft on her" she would not give up her sin. She was trying to coerce her into being good. This is not God's way. He calls, he challenges, he points out the consequences of sin, but he does not coerce.

Genuineness

To be genuine means to be oneself with another person. A genuine person does not assume an artificial role with the other. Jane apparently felt compelled to be a "judge" and a "prosecutor" for Mary. She did not allow herself to be just Jane, a friend to her roommate in a time of need.

Jane's failure to achieve these three qualities of a healing relationship meant that her conversation with Mary was destructive rather than healing.

Healing Comes from Listening Deeply

I want now to report what happened when we repeated the role-play but with the helper taking a listening stance. It produced very different results. Mildred played the role of Mary again with the same "script." Leonard played the role of Ed her priest-uncle. Uncle Ed had been present in Mary's life by way of frequent visits to her family as she was growing up. They had always been fond of one another. As she had grown older she would occasionally consult him on religious questions. Leonard

was instructed to attempt to develop the three qualities of a helping relationship in his role-play of Uncle Ed.

The scene starts with them seated in his office. After a few
chatty remarks about her family, Uncle Ed says:

> "Mary from the sound of your telephone call, I take it that
> you have something pretty serious to discuss."
>
> "Yes, Uncle Ed. I don't know anyone else to talk to. I'm
> scared. I don't know what to do."
>
> "You sound desperate. Can you tell me about it?"
>
> "When I first came to the city, it was all pretty new to
> me. I'd never been in a big city before. I tried really hard to
> get a good job so my parents would be proud of me. Well, I
> got this job in the advertising agency and I didn't know
> which way was up. Dan—that's my boss—was really good to
> me. He showed me the ropes: he introduced me to the right
> people and to some good clients." (She looks down at her
> hands in embarrassment.)
>
> (Uncle Ed noticing this says:) "It must be hard for you to
> talk to me about this."
>
> "Yes. I'm not very proud of what I have done. You see, we
> started going out together. He's married, but somehow I
> closed my eyes to that even though he told me he was commit-
> ted to his marriage. Well, as you can guess, one thing led to
> another. I went to the doctor today and he confirmed that I'm
> pregnant." (Tears run down her cheeks.)
>
> "That must be a shock to you."
>
> "I just can't believe it. I can't believe that it is happening
> to me. (Falteringly) And I can't talk to my folks about it.
> They're going to be so upset. (Soft sobs.) And I called Dan at
> work and he told me I'd better have an abortion."
>
> "How do you feel about that?"
>
> "I'm in a state of shock. I . . . I . . . just can't believe he
> would . . ." (Her voice trails off.)
>
> "He's not willing to take any responsibility for the baby?"
>
> "Just pay for the abortion is all. But I guess what hurts the
> most is that he is really telling me to 'get lost.' He's rejecting
> me. He didn't even want to talk to me about it. But I don't even
> want to talk to him after he said that. I don't know what I want
> to do. Just run away. But I've got no place to run to."
>
> "You're feeling pretty confused?"

"Yes, I don't know what to do. I don't have any options. I don't know what I'm going to do if I have this baby. I can't go back to work there. I don't have any money. I can't support this baby. How can I work and care for a child? How can I be a mother to this child with no father around? I don't know what to do."

"It looks pretty bleak."

(With a deep sigh.) "Yeah." (Long pause.)

"You have said several times that you don't have any options. I want us to look closely at that for a few minutes. I want to look at who and what can be of help to you. You said that you couldn't tell your parents. Is that really so?"

(Long pause, then deep sigh.) "Well . . . I don't know. I'm afraid that they are going to get real mad."

"What do you fear most about telling them?"

"Oh, I don't know. (Pause.) I'm afraid that they are going to tell me that I'm no good. Going off to the city the way I did and getting pregnant. Maybe they will say that I'm trash. They probably won't ever trust me again."

"Are you willing to risk that by telling them?"

"Maybe if you were there . . . Maybe they wouldn't get so angry with me. Would you help me tell them?"

"Yes. I will be there when you tell them. The reason I'm suggesting that you tell them is that you need all the help you can get. They will feel bad but I know them well enough to think that they will stick by you. Do you have anyone else you can talk with and depend on."

(Thoughtful pause.) "Yes. I have one close friend that I can count on."

"Good. I suggest you call her up and see if you can stay with her tonight. We'll talk to your parents tomorrow. I would like to check out one thing with you. I gather that you don't want an abortion but you just you don't know what to do if you have the baby. Is that right?"

"Yeah. Just the mention of abortion horrifies me. But I just don't know anything about being a mother."

"It's an awesome responsibility all right, but this is not the time to make important decisions. You're still in a state of shock: you're confused and scared. Our first task is to find all the support for you that we can. The more important decisions can come later. Is there anything more we need to do today?"

"Uncle! Would you say a prayer for me that I will do the right thing?"

"Sure! Let's do that together, right now." (We break off the simulation.)

In the discussion following the role-play Mildred said that in playing Mary she had learned how cornered a woman in Mary's situation feels. She said that the words *helpless, hopeless,* and *aloneness* best described what she was feeling. She said that she had learned the necessity of being heard when you are in Mary's situation. The feeling of aloneness was so gripping that it even excluded God's presence. She said, "I would put it this way: my head couldn't think, even to pray, until my heart had been heard and someone had reached out to help me." As she played the role of Mary the first time it got worse and worse and it was as though God was rejecting her. In the second role-play it gradually dissolved as Uncle Ed listened and finally it seemed as though God had heard her and had reached out to her. Only then could she think of prayer and of doing "the right thing". Until then all her energies had been taken up in self-preservation.

Review of the Elements of a Healing Conversation

After this role-play Mildred was able to "get out of the role" of Mary. She was able to leave Mary's feelings behind and to be Mildred again. The class, too, was relieved. Since the purpose of the role-plays had been to demonstrate the need to learn the principles of holding a pastoral conversation, I asked Mildred if she would tell us what of Uncle Ed's part had been helpful and what had not been.

It should be noted that I was not concerned with Mildred's and Leonard's acting ability. Rather, if this be taken as a real situation, how effective was the priest-uncle?

Regarding empathy, Mildred thought that Uncle Ed had been quite accurate in knowing how cornered, confused, and hopeless Mary felt. His understanding of how she felt enabled Mary to continue telling her story even when she found it embarrassing.

In regard to non-possessive warmth Mildred gave Uncle Ed

high marks. She said that although Mary knew that her uncle did not approve of her adulterous relationship, she never felt that he was condemning her. Furthermore, although Mary knew her uncle did not want her to have an abortion she never felt coerced by him as she had with Jane. Mildred said that as Mary she never felt that she had to win her uncle's love. It was just there no matter what she did or said.

As to genuineness, Mildred thought the uncle-priest came across as genuine. He did not "play games" with Mary: he did not assume an artificial role. He was just himself—a priest-uncle who dearly loved his niece and wanted the best for her.

As we ended the discussion of the two role-plays Mildred remarked, "I think I am beginning to believe that you are teaching us more than man-made counseling techniques, but it is still hard to believe that my listening is a divine activity." I agreed that it is hard, but urged her to pray for greater insight into this truth of her faith.

In summary:

- Pastoral listening is more than a human activity. We listen as ministers of Christ's healing love to a member of his body who is wounded. We listen in faith, out of love, and in hope. Mildred's objection that I was teaching only man-made techniques of counseling was not true. Pastoral listening is a divine activity.
- Pastoral listening is purposeful. We listen so that the supplicant may experience God as a listening God, We listen so that we may know how to minister healing to the supplicant's hurts.
- Pastoral listening is a loving and self-sacrificing service. While listening we put aside our needs and desires and place ourselves at the disposal of the supplicant.
- The relationship needed for effective pastoral listening is characterized by three qualities: accurate empathy, non-possessive warmth, and genuineness.
- In pastoral listening the minister is actively involved in helping the supplicant tell his story. The next chapter will describe this active involvement.

5.

Characteristics of a Good Pastoral Listener

The first role-play in the last chapter ended with Mary angrily storming out of the room unhelped by her roommate. Unless she finds someone else to help her Mary will probably have an abortion. In the second role-play she ends up praying with her priest-uncle that she will do the right thing. In this role-play she probably will not have an abortion. What made the difference? This chapter deals with this question.

In the last chapter I discussed three qualities that make a relationship helpful, and I pointed out that they were absent in Jane's relationship with Mary and present in Uncle Ed's. In this chapter I will discuss how these qualities get translated into action. I want to discuss such questions as: What are the characteristics of good listener? How can the listener respond helpfully to the supplicant's story? What are some important helps and obstacles to good listening?

Qualities of a Good Listener

Good listening is rare. Think for a moment of an occasion in which you tried to share with another your deepest feelings about something very important to you. Unless you were unusually fortunate, your listener quickly became disinterested and restless, and soon butted in with a concern of her own. She probably started telling you of something similar that happened to her or she may have simply changed the subject.

Why do we find it so difficult to listen to another? One reason is that listening demands a great deal of self-sacrifice. Attentive

59

listening demands that I restrain my desire to tell *my* story. This is a sacrifice because listening to another's pain stirs up memories of my own painful experiences which I have never shared with another and I find it difficult to put aside my own painful feelings and share the supplicant's pain. Or, if she is telling me about her joys, I may find envy rising up in me because I do not have this joy in my life. Yet to be a good listener, I must share her pain and rejoice over her good fortune. Learning to listen is really learning to love which means following him who said: "I have come in order that you may have life—life in all its fullness. I am the good shepherd, who is willing to die for the sheep" (Jn 10:10–11).

Another characteristic of a good listener is the ability to respect the supplicant. Only when I respect another will my listening be healing. Yet, in the ministry of prayer for healing we are sometimes called upon to minister to people that we find hard to respect. However, we can still minister effectively if we are able to respect some aspect of the supplicant's life.

Dolly was especially hard for me to like. She was never clean. She did not care for her children well. She was sexually promiscuous. When she came to me for help she was pregnant by someone other than her husband although she was still living with her husband. She was slightly retarded. She had a fierce temper and was filled with hatred for people in general. She expressed this hatred openly with foul language. I found her so unpleasant that at first I thought I couldn't minister to her. But as I thought more about her, I discovered that I could respect her intense desire to be a better person in the face of overwhelming obstacles. This degree of respect enabled me to listen with empathy to Dolly. I came to know what it was like to be Dolly overwhelmed by a world too complex for her to understand. Healing did come to her from my listening.

My difficulty with Dolly illustrates still another important characteristic of a good listener. A good listener must give up his need for the supplicant to behave, think, or talk, according to his expectations. When I am not conscious that I have set these standards, they exercise an excessive influence upon my feelings about the other person when he does not conform to my standards of behavior. Dolly did not meet my standards. She was not clean: she used foul language: she was sexually promiscuous. I found it hard to restrain my desire to reject her for these traits. But if I was to learn what it was like to be Dolly, I had to set aside my demand that she conform to my standards. Jane, in the first role-play of the last chapter, did not restrain her disapproval of Mary's behavior, so her listening was destructive rather than healing.

Serenity is a characteristic of a good listening: anxiety is a barrier to listening. Yet, listening deeply to another sometimes makes us anxious. Prayer is a good way to handle our anxiety. It focuses our attention upon Christ who gives us peace. A period of prayer before we start to listen is most helpful. Silent prayer while listening to a supplicant is a great aid in maintaining serenity: something simple that will not distract us from listening: perhaps silently saying the name of Jesus. Just the conscious awareness that Jesus is present in our company will dispel anxiety.

Helpful Responses

Our responses to the supplicant, as he tells us his story, have the power to help or hinder the supplicant in telling his story. Much good active listening can be done with a few different kinds of responses. Each kind has its own purpose. I want now to describe them and illustrate their use.

Indications of Acceptance

Responses that indicate my acceptance of the person and what she is telling me are very important. Listeners are frequently reluctant to communicate acceptance because they mistake acceptance for approval. They think that to respond in an accepting way will indicate approval of the supplicant's opinion. Indeed the listener is not required to give approval of the speaker's point of view. But note, acceptance is not approval. Uncle Ed did not approve of Mary's behavior any more than did her roommate Jane. But his responses let Mary know that he accepted her and wanted to understand how she viewed her problem. This acceptance of her enabled Mary to continue telling her story. Nor did she ever think that her uncle approved of her consideration of an abortion. Jane, on the contrary, because of her immediate expressions of disapproval, never found out how Mary felt about her situation and was of no help to her.

There are non-verbal ways of indicating our acceptance such as head nods, facial expressions, hand gestures, and postures of the body. Then there are verbal indications of acceptance, such as "yes," "I see," "uh-huh." These are so instinctive that we do not usually notice that we are using them. But we need to become conscious of them so that we may use them purposefully.

Reflective Responses

A reflective response goes beyond a mere indication of acceptance. It says back to the speaker what I have understood her to be telling me. This allows her to correct me if I have misunderstood. She may expand upon my statement if my understanding is incomplete. If I am "on target" she will continue her story, knowing that I have understood so far. When Mary said, "I went to the doctor today and he confirmed that I'm pregnant," Uncle Ed used a reflective response when he said, "That must be a shock to you." "Shock" may not have been the best word to describe what Mary felt, but it was sufficiently accurate to encourage Mary to continue. She enlarges his understanding by talking about her confusion, fear of telling her folks, and pressure from Dan to have an abortion.

Focusing Responses

A focusing response has two uses. The first is to help the supplicant keep on track with his story. Many people find it hard to tell their story in a straight-forward and concise way. When a person has lost track of the thread of her story a focusing response will help her get on track again. For example a supplicant might be telling of being sent to boarding school at an early age and experiencing this as rejection by her parents. As she tells the story she starts reminiscing about sports at the boarding school and this leads her to talk about how much she still loves sports.

The listener, realizing that the supplicant is off on an irrelevant tangent, might say something like this: "Let me interrupt here. You were telling me that you experienced being sent to boarding school as rejection by your parents. I would like to know a little more about your feelings of being rejected."

A focusing remark is also used to call a person back to an important point that he has rushed over. Uncle Ed did this with Mary. During a pause after she had told the highlights of her story and expressed her feelings, Uncle Ed said, "You have said several times that you don't have any options. I want us to look more closely at that." This helped Mary focus on who could be of help to her. She decided that possibly her parents might help. She came to recognize that her uncle was a resource, and that she could count on a close friend. Realizing she had these people to help her removed some of her feelings of helplessness and aloneness. She gained some sense of being in control once again and this stimulated her to start thinking of alternative solutions ("Uncle, will you say a prayer for me that I will do the right thing?").

Sometimes the listener finds that he needs more information than the supplicant has given him or he needs to clarify something. A direct question is a simple way to accomplish this. But there is a problem with direct questions. They must be used sparingly. Frequent use of direct questions sets up an atmosphere of interrogation. This causes passivity in the supplicant and discourages her from telling her story as she wants to. Rapport is damaged; the easy flow of dialogue will be disrupted; and both listener and supplicant will become frustrated. A better way is an indirect approach such as "Would you tell me a little more about that" or "I am not sure I understand what happened."

However, sometimes a direct question is the only sensible way to get the needed information or clarification. After Mary had said that she was afraid to tell her parents of her pregnancy Uncle Ed used the direct question, "Are you willing to risk that (her parents' disapproval) by telling them?" It would have been difficult to get that clarification in any other way. The question is really a way of asking her to make a decision. After Mary said that Dan wanted her to have an abortion, Uncle Ed asked the direct question, "How do you feel about that?" This was the simplest way to get that piece of information and did not interrupt the flow of her telling her story.

Facilitating Responses

Sometimes a supplicant will say something that implies an important feeling, meaning, or conflict but not be explicit about it. The listener needs to openly acknowledge that he has heard this, and to make a response that will encourage the supplicant to be explicit. These responses are called *facilitating* because they give the supplicant permission to talk about painful or embarrassing topics. Uncle Ed used a facilitating response when Mary showed considerable embarrassment at the beginning of telling her story. Uncle Ed said, "It must be hard for you to talk about this." Mary responds, "Yes, I'm not very proud of what I have done." This was a crucial point of the relationship between them. Rapport is in question. But Uncle Ed's open recognition of her feelings enabled her to continue her story.

Uncle Ed might have made a facilitating response to Mary's statement, "But I don't know that I even want to talk to him (Dan) after he said that (have an abortion)." Uncle Ed could have said something such as, "It sounds as though you are pretty angry at him." This would have enabled Mary to talk more about her feelings toward Dan. However, Uncle Ed felt it was more important at that moment to lead her out of her feelings of hopelessness than for her to talk about Dan. At some later time she will probably need to talk out her feelings toward Dan.

Helps to Good Listening

We converse for many different purposes. Not all conversations are intended to be healing and not all listening is intended to be ministry. But if the conversation is intended to be healing, it must be structured in order to be effective. By structured I mean that the various elements are consciously arranged according to a plan agreed upon by both minister and supplicant. For example, the conversation will take place in a determined setting, over a determined period of time, and for a specified purpose. A common misconception of structure is to confuse it with formality and rigidity. They are not the same. A pastoral conversation can be informal and flexible and still be structured.

The setting of a pastoral conversation is important, and I will discuss the setting in detail in a later chapter. So here I merely want to emphasize that attentive listening demands a place that is quiet, private, and protected from interruptions.

The element of time in pastoral listening also needs to be structured. The formality of the structure will depend upon the situation. The structuring of time for listening in a family will be less formal than that of a prayer team with a supplicant. But in both cases some structure is involved. A mother cooking an evening meal and approached by a small child who is crying needs to spend two or three minutes immediately, listening with full attention. The same woman cooking an evening meal and interrupted by a phone call from a supplicant would probably say, "I'm busy cooking dinner right now. May I call you back after dinner?" By responding in this way she is structuring the time element in a conversation so that it may be helpful. Her first priority is to her family. She could not listen to the telephoning supplicant effectively knowing that she was neglecting her family. She would become irritated and the supplicant would not get her full attention. For effective ministry there must be definite times designated for listening. No one can have a listening stance all of the time.

People will request ministry at inopportune times. We can use structuring responses to handle these. Marge's experience will illustrate how to do so. The setting is this. Marge is at home getting ready to leave soon for a dentist's appointment. Jenny, a newlywed who lives next door, comes bursting in through the back door, sobbing. She and her husband have had their first quarrel. Bob became angry because Jenny would not get up and fix breakfast for him before he went to work. After an angry exchange of bitter words, he left for work. Jenny says:

> "Marge, I have to talk to you right now. I'm so upset. Bob
> and I have had a terrible fight. I'm afraid he won't come home

tonight. He might never come back. Would you call him up at
the office and talk to him? Maybe he will listen to you."

Marge spent a few minutes finding out what happened.
Then she said:

> "Jenny, I have to leave for a dentist's appointment in ten
> minutes. But I will be back about one o'clock and could talk to
> you then. Will that work for you? I would be glad to say a short
> prayer with you before I leave."

Not only should there be a definite time for listening but the
length of time for ministry should be clearly stated. This is useful
for both the speaker and the listener. The supplicant knows how
much time he has and can pace his conversation accordingly.
The listener can give his full attention to the supplicant without
anxiety about how long the conversation will last. The story of
Marge and Jenny can illustrate how to structure the length of
time for a pastoral conversation. When Jenny comes back at one
o'clock, Marge might say, "I have an hour before the kids come
home from school. I will need to stop when they come home." A
prayer team would probably be more precise in setting a time for
ministry, say on Wednesday from 2:00 to 3:00 P.M.

Jenny's behavior in seeking help from Marge illustrates the
importance of clarifying each one's expectations of ministry. At
the moment she burst through Marge's kitchen door she did not
think of herself as asking for ministry. Nor had she reflected
upon the appropriateness of asking Marge to intervene by phon-
ing Bob. She was frightened by Bob's anger and was acting in
panic. If Marge had allowed herself to be caught up in Jenny's
panic and neglected to clarify Jenny's, and her own, expectations,
the result would have been disappointment and frustration for
both of them and ineffective ministry to Jenny.

A person requesting ministry will always have expectations
of how the team will help her. These expectations are usually
vague, and the person is seldom conscious of them. The team
also will have expectations of the kind of help they are willing to
give. These need to be clearly defined and conscious because the

team is responsible for working out with the supplicant a mutually acceptable agreement about the ministry to be given. The agreement will include such items as: the kind of help the team will give; how available the team will be to the supplicant; the length of time and frequency of ministry. This will be done at the beginning of ministry, but further clarification will be needed as ministry proceeds.

Some supplicants' expectations of help will conform to the team's. They want someone to listen to them, perhaps help them think of a solution, and usually pray with them. Others will have expectations of help vastly different than the team's. Jenny wanted Marge to call up her husband and straighten him out. Being a next door neighbor, Jenny expected that she could drop in any time she wanted for ministry. Marge had a different set of expectations about the help she was willing to give. She had other obligations and was only willing to do ministry at scheduled times. Jenny may have expected that Marge's ministry would be available to her as long as she lived next door. Marge would not want to foster Jenny's dependency upon her and would only be willing to minister to her for a limited period—say four or five times.

If Marge does not bring these differences into the open and come to some mutual agreement with Jenny, the ministry will likely end in conflict and hurt feelings. How does Marge do this?

When Jenny returns in the afternoon Marge will help Jenny tell her story. She would then ask, "How can I be of help to you, Jenny?"

"Would you call Bob and talk to him. Tell him not to be so demanding. Maybe he would listen to you."

"Let's look at that for a moment. If I did that he would feel that I'm butting in and that you put me up to it. I'm afraid it would just make things worse between the two of you. What I would be willing to do is to help you think of how *you* can talk to him about this problem."

If Jenny agrees that this will be helpful, Marge might then say,

"I can see you tomorrow at one for an hour. If you need more time, I could see you three more times and then we would re-evaluate your need for ministry. Is that agreeable to you?"

Beginning ministers are frequently embarrassed to discuss expectations about ministry with a supplicant. I remember myself as a young priest in a pastoral training program telling my advisor that it embarrassed me to talk about expectations with a supplicant: it made me seem cold and impersonal, and I wanted to appear friendly. My advisor responded, "If you don't love your supplicants enough to do what is right for them you should quit being a minister." That was hard for me to hear but it has been a guiding principle for me ever since.

The beginning minister is embarrassed in working out an agreement because he is not used to a different and new way of relating to people. In social situations we are usually more indirect and leave things vague. But that will not work in ministry. Working out details is a loving thing to do. Supplicants are freed from anxiety by knowing what they can expect from us. We, the ministers, are freed from the fear that too much will be asked of us. Without a clear agreement the ministry will almost certainly end in dissatisfaction for both supplicants and ministers. I cannot emphasize too strongly how important agreements are for effective ministry.

Confidentiality

The supplicant will always expect confidentiality of the minister or team even if she does not mention it. The team should take the initiative in discussing this expectation. They should explain their understanding of confidentiality and explicitly promise to maintain it. But even if it isn't promised the team is nevertheless obliged to keep secret everything learned about the supplicant, or even about others, from the ministry.

Confidentiality is a sacred obligation. The information we receive during ministry is not ours to give away. It has been given to us as a sacred trust only because we are standing in the place of Jesus. We must not share it with friends or even with our spouses. We should not even disclose that someone has come to us for ministry.

Any violation of confidentiality is disastrous to the entire body of Christ. It destroys trust not just in the ministry of the one who violates confidentiality, but in all ministry. If people even suspect that their confidence will be betrayed they will be reluctant to seek ministry, and this deprives them of the abundant life that Jesus offers.

Obstacles To Good Listening

Anxiety greatly hinders one's effectiveness as a pastoral listener. Glenda's experience illustrates how anxiety arising from feelings of incompetence can hinder us. Glenda, a beginning student in our training program, was reporting her first experience of team ministry to her teammates during a ministry review session.

"I was so nervous that I started to sweat when the supplicant came into the room. That embarrassed me and I became even more nervous. I hoped the supplicant wouldn't notice. I forgot her name as soon as she said it. I didn't hear a thing she said the first few minutes. I kept trying to remember what we were supposed to say and do in the first session with a supplicant. I knew I was suppose to listen but I couldn't. I was too worried. I kept thinking, 'What if the leader calls on me to pray for her? What will I say? I don't even know what she wants prayer for.' I sure hoped that our team leader knew what to do. Finally I got hold of myself and started to pray silently. After a little while I calmed down and then I started to hear what she was saying. She'd had some terrible experiences in her childhood. Our leader was doing a good job of helping her tell her story. The leader didn't call on me but at the end of our time with her I was able to say a brief prayer asking God to give her peace."

Glenda's experience is common for beginning ministers. In the presence of the supplicant her self-confidence ebbed away. She felt awkward and unskilled. She couldn't remember the things she had already learned. She worried about what she might be called upon to do. These very anxieties prevented her from even listening to the supplicant. She hoped her teammates knew what to do.

Everyone has these feelings in the beginning. The most effective remedy is experience. But even in this first session Glenda was finally able to pray briefly. She remembered to pray silently and this calmed her. Being a member of a team gave her time to get hold of herself. This is an important advantage of team ministry.

But in discussing her experience with her teammates, Glenda was doing something else to reduce anxiety. She was reflecting on her ministry in a purposeful way. Through it she will learn what areas need more attention. Her teammates will point out abilities that she can't see in herself. Thus she will learn from her experience, become more skillful, and grow in confidence.

Another obstacle to good listening is to misconceive the task of the listener. There are a number of common misconceptions held by pastoral workers. For example, Jane, in the first role-play in the previous chapter, was not able to listen because she thought her task was to "set Mary right" about moral issues.

Another misconception is to think that *I* must solve the supplicant's problem. I experienced this with Marie who came to me for ministry. She said, "My daughter is going to give up her faith to marry a man who hates all religions. I wish you would talk to her. I know she would listen to you." Marie continued talking but I was no longer hearing her. My thoughts were frozen. At first I felt something like panic, then dread, then anger. I caught myself about to say, "I have to go now, but let's pray about that." I knew that I did not "have to go now." What was going on with me? I was about to terminate this meeting with Marie and to leave her unhelped.

I still could not "hear" Marie but I restrained my impulse to terminate. I started to pray silently for guidance from the Holy Spirit. I mentally repeated the name of Jesus slowly in rhythm with my breathing. Quickly my feelings subsided and I was able to connect with Marie's story. All of this took less than a minute. I said to Marie, "I really wish I could talk your daughter out of her decision, but I can't. She would resent my interference. It would only make matters worse. Let's see what else I might do to be of help." Together we worked out a way that I could minister to Marie's needs.

The problem was that I temporarily "bought into" Marie's desire for me to solve her problem. I felt that I had to do something to stop the daughter. But I couldn't solve Marie's problem. The daughter would not "listen to me" as the mother hoped. I knew from past experience that a clergyman can't talk a young woman in love out of her choice of a mate. Because I felt that I had to solve the problem and yet couldn't do so, I felt panic. Then I became angry at being put into that situation. (In reality I had put myself into it, but I blamed Marie.) And to get out of the situation I was going to terminate our meeting and leave Marie unhelped.

The focus had shifted away from Marie onto me. Because I was anxious I reacted with panic and hostility. Now Marie had two problems: the one she came with, and me. If I had abruptly terminated our meeting, as I was tempted to do, she would have left unhelped and feeling rejected. But I was able to "catch on" in time to remedy the situation.

What enabled me to "catch on"? First of all I really did know the proper role of a pastoral listener. And the practice of reflecting upon my ministry has taught me to be alert to my feelings. My inappropriate feelings alerted me that something was wrong. I suspect also that the Spirit may have had something to do with alerting me. I know for certain that praying the name of Jesus brought peace and clarity. This allowed me to use a structuring response that freed both of us from a misconception of ministry. Then I was able to be truly helpful to Marie.

Another misconception is to think that as a pastoral listener I ought to be able to answer insoluble questions raised by the supplicant. The memory of one such occasion is still vivid and painful for me. I had only been ordained a short while when I was asked to minister to a patient dying painfully of cancer. During my first visit she said to me: "Why doesn't God care about me?

Why did this have to happen to me?" I didn't want her to think badly of God. I wanted her to experience God's love for her, so I tried to give a theological explanation of evil. It did not satisfy her, so I tried harder to convince her of its truth. The more I tried the more she resisted. We ended up in a theological argument. I was no help to her. She did not need a lesson in theology: she needed me to be God's ear while she told him how angry she was about her pain. If she had felt heard by God, through my listening, she would have been ready to listen to him through Scripture, prayer, and our conversation.

In this and the previous chapter I have emphasized that the ministry of listening is hard work and demands disciplined self-sacrifice. But it is also a rewarding ministry. We are privileged that people entrust us with so much of their lives. We see so much of God working in the lives of others. I find that through this ministry God reveals more of himself to me than in any other way. I thank God for allowing me to minister as a listener. I pray that all of us who minister healing prayer may grow in our ability to listen with God's loving heart.

I have discussed how to minister healing prayer as a team and the all-important art of pastoral listening. In the next chapter I will discuss the four kinds of hurts that humans are subject to, how they are interrelated and how to bring healing to them.

SECTION THREE

HEALING THE HUMAN HURTS

6

Four Kinds of Wounds
and Four Kinds of Healing

I walked into Room 231 of the Burn Trauma Unit. All I could see of Reuben were his eyes and mouth. His head, chest, arms and hands were totally wrapped in gauze. The head nurse of the burn unit had asked me to visit Reuben. She said he was badly burned, in serious condition, and was uncooperative and verbally abusive to the nurses. I was greeted with: "Who the hell are you?"

"Fr. Thomas, the hospital chaplain."

"I don't want to see no goddam chaplain".

My heart went out to Reuben. He was so helpless and miserable.

"You must be in a lot of pain," I said.

"Pain! Are you kidding? My whole body is on fire. But that's not the worst of it. These damn nurses soak me in a tub and scrub me down with a bristle brush twice a day. Those bitches couldn't care less how much it hurts. I always thought I was tough but it's more than *I* can take." His voice broke.

"How did it happen?"

"It was so stupid. The foreman told me to weld a gasoline tank. 'It's safe. There's no gas in it,' he said. Like an idiot I believed him and did what he said and it exploded in my face. Now here I am, flat on my back in this goddam hospital and I probably won't ever work again. That is, if I live. His voice broke again and he quit talking.

"How is your family taking it?", I asked.

"Damned if I know."

"Haven't they visited you?"

"Hell no! I told 'em to keep the wife and kids out of here. If

she saw me without this gauze on she would freak out. I'm ugly."
He paused, and then said: "I suppose I'll be ugly the rest of my
life, and I don't think she can love me looking like that."

He was silent a minute and then added: "My wife's got
enough to worry about right now. How's she gonna make the
payments on the house and car? On top of that, I don't dare think
about the medical bill."

A nurse interrupted us saying it was time for Reuben's treatment. I said: "I'll see you again tomorrow." He responded: "Don't
bother. There ain't nothing you can do for me. God's getting even
with me."

"What for?"

"Not being a good Catholic."

"What's that mean?"

"Oh stuff like cussin' a lot, and not going to church".

I said that I would like to visit him anyway and finish our
conversation. He gave me a reluctant "O.K."

Ministering to Reuben forced me to remember the Hebrews'
notion of the unity of the human person which we moderns have
largely lost. We think of ourselves as composed of parts: body and
soul; mind and matter. This is understandable. We are surrounded by machines that have parts that we can remove, repair
or replace. This leads us to think of the human person in the
same way. Organ transplants, commonplace in today's medical
practice, reinforces this way of thinking.

But we humans are not machines: we are not composed of
removable parts. I cannot accurately say, without further qualifi-
cation, that my soul is more important than my body. There are
no real "parts" in a human person. I am a single living unit—but
such a complex unit that I need a simple way of talking about
myself. I do this by identifying aspects of my personality and
calling them "parts." Thus in religious circles I may speak of
having a body and a soul. And I may say that my soul is more
important than my body. But this is just a shorthand way of
communicating the complicated truth that my relationship with
God is the most important aspect of my human existence. In this
book I will sometimes use this convenient way of speaking, but in
doing so I do not intend to deny the essential unity of the human

person. I will, for example, talk about the need of healing for our physical, emotional, spiritual and relational parts.

I want now to identify what I mean by each of these "parts" and to illustrate how they can be hurt.

- Physical: skin, blood, muscles, bones, organs.
- Emotional: joy, fear, anxiety, anger, resentments.
- Spiritual: the mind and the will; the religious responses of the human person.
- Relational: the kinds of relationships we have with our environment, with other human beings, and with God.

Physical

Physical ailments are the easiest for us to understand. A single glance at Reuben told me he was physically hurt. These can be caused by injury, by infection and disease, or by congenital defects.

Emotional

We may not be as familiar with the idea of wounded emotions, but when our emotions feel pain they can cause us to react in distorted and destructive ways. Deprivation and trauma are two common causes of emotional woundedness. A child raised without sufficient displays of love—not cuddled enough, not touched enough—is emotionally deprived. Later in life, this child will find it difficult to believe in his own worth. He may find it difficult to love others freely and openly. A sexually abused child is wounded emotionally by trauma. This person, as an adult, will find it difficult to react with appropriate sexual pleasure until the wound has been healed.

On the other hand, healthy emotions enable us to react to life's events in ways that will achieve our purpose in life. For example, fear is the proper reaction to a dangerous situation. It alerts us so that we might act in a way to preserve our life. Reuben's fear that he might not recover was a proper response to his life-threatening burns.

Spiritual

Our spiritual dimension is closely connected to our being created in God's image. He has given us a mind—the ability to know as he does: and a will—the ability to make choices as he does. Our spiritual dimension can also be wounded. Spiritual woundedness results in a *falling away from our likeness to God.* This woundedness will happen when our minds are given wrong or distorted information, especially about spiritual things. For example, many people have been taught to see God as a harsh and tyrannical monster—someone out to get them. This is the way Reuben felt. His misinformation prevented him from receiving God's love or in giving his love to God.

Spiritual woundedness also happens when our wills are affected so that we can no longer choose freely. Spiritual deprivation and spiritual trauma are causes of spiritual woundedness. For example, a child who is not taught the basics of relgion—God is a loving parent, Jesus is our Savior, how to pray—is spiritually deprived, and will suffer the negative consequences of it as an adult. He may never come to know God and be a religious person. An example of spiritual trauma would be a boy who, at an early age, is introduced by his criminal father into the world of organized crime and taught that it is an ideal way of life. It is very unlikely that he will ever extricate himself from a life of crime.

Relational

We live in an age that is keenly aware of relationships, but we sometimes think of them as optional. The truth is that relationships are not optional for humans. From birth to death, we are dependent on other humans for our very existence. An infant is totally dependent on relationships for survival. If it were possible for an infant to be cared for by a machine—to be kept warm, to be fed, to be kept clean, but with no human contact—that infant would die. The adult person, while not quite so vulnerable, also needs relationships with other humans in order to become the person God intends. When relationships become distorted or destructive, we suffer the consequences. Husband-wife, parent-child, teacher-student, and friend-friend are some of the common human relationships that can become destructive. But, of course the list of possibilities is endless. It can include our relationship to God, to the body of Christ, to the deceased, to animals, and even to our physical environment.

The sources of hurtful relationships are too numerous and too complex to be explained in this brief overview of the four kinds of wounds. A later chapter will discuss these sources in detail. But Reuben's way of relating to his nurses and to his wife illustrates one common source—immaturity. By that I mean that his ability to establish constructive relationships was not fully developed. His blaming of the nurses for the pain he suffered during the treatment for his burns and his verbal abuse of them was not a mature way to handle an admittedly difficult relationship. His refusal to see his wife because of his disfigurement was not a mature way of dealing with his fear of losing her love.

We also have a relationship to the spiritual realm, that is, to God, to his angels, and also to demons. Each of these relationships can become distorted and destructive. For example we can attempt to manipulate God to do our bidding by practicing certain rituals. We can establish destructive relationships with the world of evil spirits by seeking power through the use of occult practices. Or evil spirits can victimize us by harassment or by temptation.

Interrelatedness of Human Hurts

This has been a brief overview of the four kinds of wounds we humans universally suffer. Later I will cover each kind in greater detail and discuss how they can be ministered to.

Having talked about the woundedness of four aspects of our nature, I now want to emphasize the essential unity of the human person. Because we are a single unit with no separable parts, a wound in one dimension means that the *entire* human person is wounded in some way. The hurt in one part may be so minor that it is scarcely noticeable in the other aspects of the human person. A tiny splinter in my little finger will hardly have any noticeable effect on my emotional, spiritual, or relational parts. But Reuben's third degree burns over fifty percent of his body had profound repercussions in all the other aspects of his life. His emotional life was greatly affected. Understandably, he was fearful. Feelings of guilt were stirred up. His spiritual life was troubled as illustrated by his statement: "God's getting even with me." Reuben's relationships were disturbed. He was name-calling his foreman and the nurses who were caring for him. He shut out his wife because he feared losing her love.

Reuben's predicament illustrates the connectedness of four aspects of our human nature. It is not the body that is wounded, or the spirit that is wounded. It is the whole person who is hurt. Sometimes hurts sustained in one's emotional life can cause illness to the body. For example, a hard-driving, over-achieving executive may suffer a heart attack. To be healed she may need to review her set of values and the way she relates to others. Her physician may rightly consider spiritual counseling a valid part of treatment for her heart attack.

Another story, briefer than that of Reuben, may illustrate this essential unity of our being and the connectedness of these four kinds of wounds. A friend of mine had rheumatic fever, an infection of the heart muscles, when he was a seventh grader. He related:

> "I had to drop out of school and I remained in bed for nearly a year. But the illness affected not just my heart; it caused me emotional pain too. I suffered from loneliness. I felt imprisoned in my bed. I would hear my classmates go past the house after school, and feel left out of their social life. I worried about my education. A teacher came to tutor me but I feared I would fail and would be humiliated by having to repeat the seventh grade."

The rheumatic fever also contributed to spiritual disorders. He became very anxious about his relationship to God. He said:

> "I felt God was punishing me for something I had done and wondered what it might be. 'Could it be the thoughts I've been having about sex?' I was frightened. When the priest came to bring me Holy Communion I felt terribly guilty, but I was too embarrassed to tell the priest my worries."

His illness disrupted his relationships to family members: He continues his story.

"My sickness made me self-centered, irritable, and not very pleasant to be with. I remember taking it out on Bobby, my little brother. He was standing by the bed teasing me. I couldn't get out of bed, but I made a small slingshot with a rubber band and shot a steel paper clip. It hit my brother on the cheek just below the eye and caused a slight wound. When Mom found out about it she became furious at me for doing something so dangerous. She yelled at me. I cried and felt hurt and rejected by her. As a result I had a physical setback that took me weeks to recover from."

He concluded his story by saying: "It wasn't my heart that was sick. It was *me* that was sick, and I was sick *all over*."

Healing Our Woundedness

It's good for ministers of healing prayer to be aware of all of the remedies God has given us for the healing of our woundedness. Categorizing these many means of healing makes it easier to remember them.

Natural Remedies: { e.g., medicine, counseling, listening, instruction.

Supernatural Remedies: { May be administered by any Christian, e.g., prayer, scripture, sacramentals.
Administration reserved to ordained minister, e.g., certain blessings, sacraments.

Each one of the four kinds of human hurts can be healed by either natural or supernatural remedies or by a combination of both.

The natural means of healing are part of God's general plan

of creation. God has given them to us precisely because we are his creatures and so they are available to all human beings. Medical treatment, psychiatric care, marriage and family counseling, knowledge of nutrition and exercise, listening to another person, are all natural ways of healing.

But we are more than creatures of God. Through faith in Christ and baptism we are his children. He has adopted us into his family and we share in his divine nature. (This is the meaning of supernatural. We are living a life beyond our natural human powers.) And so God as a loving Father has given us means of healing that are in accord with our new nature. These are the supernatural ways of healing. Because God has given us these means—the natural as well as the supernatural—we need to use them in full trust that he will care for our every need. My work with Reuben illustrates how natural and supernatural remedies can be combined and applied to particular kinds of hurts.

Natural and Supernatural Remedies Combined

Reuben's primary hurt was physical—severe burns. For this he was receiving the proper medical treatment: medicines and daily "scrubbing" procedures to remove the dead tissue and to promote new growth. His body responded well and started to heal quickly. Later there were skin grafts and cosmetic surgery. As a result, there were no permanent scars on his face and only minor ones on his arms and body. A psychiatric social worker helped deal with the fears that his disfigurement would repulse his wife and children. He finally allowed them to visit him.

With the family present I administered the anointing of the sick and Holy Communion. This family celebration did much to heal family relationships as well as his body. Their visible signs of love for him allayed his fears that his disfigured body repulsed them. After several visits, I explained prayer for healing and he allowed me to pray for physical healing and later for inner healing of the fear and anxiety resulting from the accident. This, with the psychiatric counseling, helped and he soon became more hopeful about his situation.

The spiritual dimension was the most difficult to heal. After many meetings Reuben trusted me enough to tell me that he thought God was a harsh and punitive person. I encouraged him to talk more about this and when he was ready to hear a different point of view, I read to him the story of the father and the prodigal son. Reuben broke into sobs and told me that his own father had been tyrannical and physically abusive. He had frequently beaten Reuben severely for small infractions of household rules. He spoke vehemently of how he still hated his father. I prayed with him for inner healing of these terrible experiences a number of times. He finally experienced healing of his memories and was able to forgive his father, now dead. He made use of the sacrament of reconciliation and experienced forgiveness and peace. After this his negative attitudes toward God changed quickly and he became quite interested in reading the Bible.

Soon after this, he was discharged from the hospital but continued treatment as an outpatient. I did not see him for a few months. One day I heard a knock on my office door and looked up to see Reuben standing in the doorway. He had a big grin on his face.

"Hi, Father," he said. "I came by to tell you my treatments are finished. I'm back on the job and doing okay. My face came out pretty good, didn't it? Hardly any marks at all. I just want to say thanks for everything."

Remedies Combine for Spiritual Healing

Another story will illustrate the use of the natural and supernatural means of healing when the hurt is primarily spiritual.

I reached the end of the cafeteria line with my tray of food and looked around the dining room for a place to sit. I noticed Mark sitting alone by the window. His dignity and his bearing made me want to know him better. I wove my way between the round tables to his. He smiled and motioned to a chair. "Would you like to sit down, Father?" He extended his hand to the place across from him.

"How is the retreat going for you?" I asked.

He leaned back in his chair and looked out at the beautiful grounds of the retreat house. The atmosphere was one of deep serenity. He turned his head to me and with a smile said,

"It's incredible. I can hardly believe I'm in a place like this. Two years ago, I was traveling with a whole different crowd. Then I could not even have imagined this way of life existed. In my whole life I had never even heard about God except as a cuss word or as a joke. But that was two years ago. I am so happy to be on this retreat."

He went back to his food. I said:

"Mark, when we finish eating would you be willing to share your story with me? I'm intrigued. But I am more than curious. I believe that your experience would give me a better understanding of spiritual healing."

Later Mark told me that when he was twenty-two he joined a motorcycle gang widely known for its lawlessness. He had fully participated in its violent way of life. Two years later he had a serious motorcycle accident and while recovering in a Catholic hospital he was visited by the chaplain. He was favorably impressed by the friendly attitude of the chaplain and the religious sisters who nursed him. These contacts made him curious about the Catholic religion and he started asking the chaplain religious questions. Before he left the hospital he asked how he might learn more about the Catholic faith. The chaplain arranged for him to have a course of instructions. Through this instruction he had a conversion and at the end of the course he asked to be baptized in the Catholic Church.

At one point in our conversation I asked Mark why he'd joined the motorcycle gang.

"Simply because I didn't have anything else to believe in or anything else better to do. I had to do something to fill that terrible emptiness. When I discovered in the inquiry class that there was a God and that he loved me enough to send his own Son to find me I was dumbfounded. It was too good to be true.

It took me a long time to believe that this could be true. But once I could believe, I wanted nothing else but to follow the way of life Jesus gave us."

The ministry of spiritual healing demands great sensitivity to the condition of the recipient and a thorough command of the many means of healing at the disposal of the minister. Mark told me that twice he had been approached by a Christian filled with evangelistic zeal who warned him: "You will die in your sins and go to everlasting damnation unless you repent and accept Jesus as your Savior." Mark said: "This had no meaning to me. I merely dismissed it as the ravings of a religious nut."

Both the chaplain and the nursing sisters showed sensitivity. In his first visits the chaplain did not talk about Mark's spiritual condition until he indicated his openness to discussing this. Considering the stage Mark was at, the religious sisters' loving care of him contributed more to healing his spiritual woundness than would any talk about the state of his soul. The beginning of Mark's spiritual healing, then, started with the natural means of ordinary human friendliness and loving nursing care. This healing was continued through the course of instruction that he took.

Now supernatural means of healing enter into the picture. The word of God, communicated sensitively and in a carefully planned sequence, changed Mark. The course of instruction filled his mind with correct knowledge of God and gave his will the ability to make some new choices. Mark made an important choice. He decided to respond to God's word and to change his way of life. He asked for baptism and he received the sacraments of confirmation and the Eucharist. After his conversion he found that he still had many un-Christian attitudes left over from his earlier way of life. Here the ministry of healing prayer was used. He asked members of a prayer group to pray for the healing of these. He also found the sacrament of reconciliation helpful in strengthening his will to do the right things. Mark was attending the retreat because his confessor had told him that retreats are a powerful aid in healing spiritual woundedness. Mark reported that the Eucharist was removing the terrible emptiness he had felt from his teen years.

I am grateful to Mark for telling me his story. His healing was the most thoroughgoing spiritual healing I have encountered, and I learned much from him.

Combined Remedies for Healing Relationships

Another story, that of Irene, is a good illustration of God healing wounded family relationships through both natural and supernatural means of healing.

My two teammates and I had just finished a workshop at a charismatic renewal conference when a smiling woman approached us. She greeted us with, "I'm Irene, and I want you to know how much you have done for me and my family. You have changed our lives."

She then told us that two years earlier, at a similar conference, she had heard our presentation, "The Power of Affirmation as a Way of Life," and she said:

> "During your presentation I had to face the fact that I had come to the conference to get away from Robbie, my eleven year old son. He and I had been in constant conflict since he was an infant, and it was wrecking our entire family. As I listened to your presentation I realized that I had never affirmed Robbie in his entire life. All I had done was 'put him down.' I felt so bad that I started to cry right in the middle of your presentation. I asked Jesus to forgive me and promised him that I would become an affirming person. While you were talking, I started to make a list of things I could affirm in Robbie. I didn't even wait until I got home. I called him on the phone and told him I loved him and mentioned one of his special qualities. He was shocked, but after a while he said, 'I love you, too, Mom.' "

Irene told us that when she returned home she started a program of affirming Robbie and the other family members. By the end of the second year, the family was so completely transformed that Irene's husband decided to come to the conference to see for himself what had transformed the family so completely.

An ordinary lecture and the very human practice of affirmation started the process of healing this family's wounded relationships. But Irene very wisely used every means of healing at her disposal.

Irene told us that she had sought prayer to heal her part in the conflict. She had not wanted another child, and when she became pregnant with Robbie, she had turned her resentment upon him.

She made frequent use of the sacrament of reconciliation to take away the effects of the sin of resentment and anger that had accumulated over the years. She prayed each day that the Lord would help her call upon the grace of the sacrament of matrimony. She found that the grace of the sacrament was a powerful help to her; it helped her to make Christ's love real to the entire family.

We humans are marvelously complex creations of God. We are meant to share in his joy. But we are so vulnerable: so many "bad things" happen to us. The Father wants us well and so has given us, through Christ, many remedies to heal our ills. Healing is a ministry so dear to the heart of Jesus that he commissions us to continue his healing presence in the world. He would have us learn by prayer, study, and experience how better to make his healing presence felt by all in need.

7.

Healing Physical Hurts

At breakfast the prior asked me to come to his office when I had finished eating. When I was seated he said to me, "Fr. Anthony told me that he wanted you to preach the homily at his funeral Mass. How do you feel about that?" I knew what the prior was thinking. Fr. Anthony had died the previous night, after six months of struggling with cancer and I had ministered prayer for healing to him during this time. In fact he had died just minutes after our last visit together. The prior was wondering if I was feeling that I was being asked to bury one of my "failures"? I appreciated the prior's sensitivity to my situation, but in fact I did not feel that Fr. Anthony was "one of my failures."

I answered, "Fr. Prior, I *want* to preach the homily. I feel it will be the completion of my ministry to Tony." Two months earlier I could not have said that. Then I *was* feeling like a failure. But my recent ministry to a dying Tony had radically changed my understanding of healing prayer.

Fr. Anthony was only forty when he died. He and I were members of the same religious order and, for the past three years, of the same prayer group.

The prayer group had only recently learned about prayer for healing and had started the practice of praying over supplicants at the end of the general prayer meeting. So when Fr. Anthony received his medical diagnosis he asked us to pray over him for healing. We were shocked by the news of cancer and for the first few weeks we prayed over him fervently at every opportunity. During these times of prayer there were several prophecies that he would be healed. The community, rather frantically, I thought, exhorted Fr. Anthony to have expectant faith that he would be healed. It was obvious that we expected a dramatic and instantaneous healing and we became confused when it did not happen. The prayer for Fr. Anthony became chaotic and undisciplined as the weeks went by.

Finally I and two of the leaders held a meeting with Fr. Anthony and discussed why healing was not happening. We decided that something else needed to happen first. We had heard of "healing of memories" and decided we should pray for that first. We had also heard that unforgiveness blocks healing so we would also help Fr. Anthony look for areas of unforgiveness. We decided that only the three of us would be the ones to pray with Fr. Anthony on a regular basis and we would do so in private. Fr. Anthony was in agreement with this arrangement. This was in the early days of the healing ministry and we were inexperienced.

This new approach proved fruitful. Fr. Anthony surfaced many painful memories that were healed. He also openly looked at a seriously wounded relationship with an older brother. They had not spoken since the death of their father. At that time they had quarreled over disposing of the family income.

But in spite of all this ministry Fr. Anthony's physical condition worsened. I told the team that I thought we needed to help him face the possibility of death. They agreed reluctantly but asked me to speak with him privately first. Fr. Anthony was now confined to bed most of the time. The next day I visited him and gingerly brought up the subject. "Tony, have you considered the possibility that you might not be healed?"

He responded, "Yes the doctor has talked openly about death as a real possibility, but I've tried not to dwell on it. I've not wanted to think negative thoughts."

I said, "I think we should take a two track approach. Complete healing is still one possibilty; another is death. Let's pursue both." Tony said that it would be a relief to be able to talk openly about death, and that it had been hard to avoid these thoughts.

Fr. Anthony had several things he wanted to discuss. He wanted to be reconciled with his older brother. After some discussion he decided to telephone his brother and ask him to come to visit him. He was also feeling sad that he would not be able to continue to help his widowed sister raise her three small children. He was very close to her and he had been an active father-figure to her children. He decided to make a series of audio tapes that they could listen to when they were older. He wanted to tell them things about himself and about their family history. He was chairman of the theology department in the seminary and he wanted to get the records in good order so that someone else could take over in the event of his death.

During this time we continued to pray for healing, but one day he said, "Please don't pray for physical healing anymore. It's too hypocritical. I can no longer believe that God is going to heal me." I sensed the bitterness in his voice and mentioned it. He said, "Yes, I'm bitter. Others have received healing through my prayer; why doesn't Jesus heal me? He's abandoned me to my pain." At this he started to cry and I started to cry with him. He had voiced a question that had troubled all of us—one that we had tried to ignore.

It was a time of spiritual struggle for all of us. Why were our prayers for healing not being heard? At our next prayer time the team discussed this openly with Fr. Anthony. Although several possibilities occurred to us none of them rang true. I suggested that we spend the entire session praying about our lack of success. Fr. Anthony agreed but without any enthusiasm. We read several Scripture verses in which God promised his continued presence, and then prayed with them in mind. I summed up the prayer time with this prayer:

> "Father, your son Anthony is sick. While Jesus walked this earth he healed all who came to him. We have followed his command to lay hands upon the sick and heal them. We are puzzled that Fr. Anthony is not healed. Father, you seem so silent, so far away. Please make your loving presence known to Anthony and to us."

Our prayer ended with a profound sense of God's silence.

The next day Fr. Anthony was a changed person. He was eager to tell us what had happened. During the night when he was in considerable pain he cried out with bitterness to God, "You don't even care that I hurt. Why don't you do something for me?" He then had an image of himself as a small child when he had been critically ill with a kidney disease. In the image he was in the hospital and his human father was standing by the bed. A concerned physician and a nurse were also there. His father was sobbing with grief. Then, in the image, his human father was replaced by God as Father who was also sobbing with grief, feeling very helpless in the face of Fr. Anthony's suffering. At that moment Fr. Anthony *felt* God's compassion for him, and he *knew* that God had done everything he possibly could for him, including sending his Son Jesus to heal him. Tony was so graphic in his description that we could feel what he felt. Although he did not have an intellectual "answer" to the question of why he was not being healed, he now "knew" that God cared.

Our ministry to Fr. Anthony was a turning point in my understanding of the ministry of healing prayer. It forced me to give up the simplistic understanding of healing that says, "You just pray with faith and God heals." It caused me to undertake the effort, which still continues, to penetrate the divine mystery involved in healing. I discovered that with healing, as with all divine mysteries, the more one learns the deeper the mystery becomes.

After his experience of God's compassion, Fr. Anthony wanted to pray more but was hindered by the stupefying effects of his pain medication. He discussed with the physician the feasibility of discontinuing the pain medication. The physician was not very encouraging. He told Fr. Anthony that the withdrawal symptoms would be severe and without medication the pain would be unbearable. Fr. Anthony asked us to pray specifically that he could do without this medication. We did so and Fr. Anthony was able to do without pain medicine completely with no withdrawal symptoms and very little pain. After this he spent most of his time in prayer and was almost constantly in God's presence. He told us, "This is the best time I have ever had with God."

Toward the end he asked me if I would preach at his funeral Mass. He said that he knew many members of the prayer group would be hurt and confused because, in spite of our ministry and of the prophecies that he would be healed, he had died. Fr. Anthony asked that in my preaching I make clear that although a battle had been lost, a victory had been won. Jesus had not been defeated; he had won the victory for which he had died and risen. I agreed to preach the homily as he wished. Later I will share what I said in this homily, but before I do so I want to talk about some ideas basic to a deeper understanding of the mystery of physical healing.

Health and Healing

Perhaps the most basic concept is that of the religious meaning of "health." Physicians generally use the word "health" to indicate a lack of disease of the human organism. They use "healing" to mean any intervention by physical, chemical or surgical methods to overcome disease when it has afflicted the human organism.

But the *religious* meaning of "health" is quite different: it means wholeness—the very wholeness of God himself. Jesus proclaimed this message: the human person, wounded by sin, is being called into God's own wholeness. And the *religious* meaning of "healing" is God's activity, in Christ, bringing us into that wholeness.

The religious meaning of "healing" is the ongoing process of transformation of the person into a new reality. This transformation is the work of Christ who has bestowed on us the gift of sharing in the Father's divine nature. St. Paul expresses this transformation in this way:

> "When anyone is joined to Christ he is a new being: the old is gone, the new has come" (2 Cor 5:15–17).

St. John expresses the same truth using the idea of a new birth:

> "I tell you the truth: no one can see the kingdom of God unless he is born again" (Jn 3:3).

> "Some however did receive him and believed in him; so he gave them the right to become God's children . . . God himself was their Father" (Jn 1:12–13).

Consequently, physical healing is a part, but only a part, of God's mending of the human person, transforming her into the new creation she is intended to be. The total transformation includes also a mending of the the emotional, spiritual and relational aspects of the person. From a religious perspective physical health is not an end of itself apart from the transformation of the total person into the divine reality. For the Christian, wellness is that state of being that enables him to travel on his spiritual journey toward God's wholeness.

It is important to keep this firmly in mind when talking about praying for physical healing. The healing team's task is to proclaim, to inaugurate and to portray God's call to become a new creation. Its success is not to be measured solely by overcoming disease. That is part of it, but not the totality of its success. If the team's ministry enables the supplicant, in any degree, to travel better on his spiritual journey toward God's wholeness, then the team's ministry to that degree has been successful. Thus the prayer team's ministry to Fr. Anthony was essentially successful in that it contributed to his transformation into the divine reality. Through their ministry he became more of a son of God than he would have been without it.

It is also true that the medical treatment by the physician was successful to the extent that it contributed to Fr. Anthony's ability to continue on his spiritual journey. From a purely medical understanding of "health" and "healing" both the physician's treatment and our prayer for physical healing would have been called failures. But from a religious understanding of these terms they were both essentially successful.

But even from a religious understanding of these terms we were not entirely successful. Fr. Anthony did not recover from his physical illness in this life as ideally he should have. To that degree our ministry was a failure. I say this because I want to make very clear that I am *not* saying that the supplicant should not expect healing as a result of the team's ministry. On the contrary, both team and supplicant should expect that healing will be part of God's loving response to the supplicant's need. But how this will come about is another question that we need to look at now.

How Religious Healing Works

The beginning of our ministry to Fr. Anthony was flawed by two fundamental errors. (1) Our approach was too "superspiritual" in that the focus of our attention was on dramatic results. (2) We lacked a sufficient appreciation of the organic unity of the human person. We acted as if we could separate Fr. Anthony's physical illness from all the other aspects of his humanity. Fr. Anthony's request for physical healing plunged him and us into his total spiritual journey. We were unexpectedly involved in a crisis situation in his journey of transformation into the divine reality.

Both of these errors narrowed our vision and blinded us from seeing what God was doing. We mistakenly thought our ministry was not producing results. Only out of seeming failure were we able to give up a "superspiritual" approach. This opened our minds sufficiently to start praying for healing in Fr. Anthony's emotional, spiritual and relational dimensions, as well as in the physical. An understanding of the religious meaning of "health" and "healing" would have spared all of us much anguish and confusion. But we had not yet learned this truth. We learned it by reflecting upon our "failed" ministry.

We were fortunate that Fr. Anthony took part in this reflection. His input was crucial to our understanding of what God was doing. Both Fr. Anthony and I had been trained in Thomistic theology. This was a big help. One day, after he had passed his spiritual crisis and was now experiencing God's presence, I asked him if the team had done anything that had been especially helpful. He said, "That time you wept with me when I complained to God: 'Why doesn't Jesus heal me? He's abandoned me to my pain.' In retrospect I think your weeping allowed me to experience God's compassion. I didn't realize it then, but now I think that you were God-for-me at that moment. If, in your feelings of helplessness and uselessness, you had given up on me, I might never have experienced God's compassion for me."

I asked him to think with me how we might understand this theologically. As we discussed our ministry to him we saw that we needed to return to an incarnational theology if we were to understand this ministry of healing. "Superspiritualism" overvalues God's part, and undervalues the minister's part, in the process of healing. In our ministry we had been using slogans such as, "It is God who heals; we only pray," whereas incarnational theology would say that any healing that occurs comes totally from God as source and cause of healing, and totally from the team as agents which he uses to channel his healing power. This is indeed an astounding statement and needs some explanation.

Instruments of God's Healing Power

Jesus is Lord of every part of the universe. In Colossians 1:16–17 we are told that "God created the entire universe through him and for him . . . and in union with him all things have their proper place." Thus Jesus is able to use all of created being as instruments to achieve his purposes, including healing. He uses antibiotics, chemotherapy, psychological counseling, and the natural healing forces in the human body as well as the ministry of prayer to heal a sick person. God is equally at work in the administration of an antibiotic as he is in the ministry of healing prayer. This means that we must have a certain humility about our ministry. We must respect medical science as part of God's loving care of his children.

Incarnational theology tells us, then, that in our ministry of healing prayer God chooses to use us as an instrument. I will use the field of music to illustrate what I mean. Beethoven was able to compose beautiful music in his mind. He could sit in the silence of his deafness and in his mind "hear" his music note by note. But if he were to have come out on the stage of a concert hall and just sit there "thinking" his music with no orchestra playing it, the rest of the world would never have received his gift of music. However, when he wrote out the score of the music he had composed in his mind and gave it to an orchestra to perform it is true to say that the music came totally from Beethoven as its creator, and yet it came totally from the musical instruments— empowered by human players—producing the sounds Beethoven intended.

Just as Beethoven used the musical instruments of the orchestra to give his gift of music to the world, so God uses us as living instruments to give his gift of wholeness to all of creation.

However, there are some important differences between a human instrument and a musical instrument. As human instruments, we are endowed with intelligence and free will. When God uses us as an instrument he respects our nature as he created it. He does not use us as if we were lifeless puppets. So even though we are instruments in God's hands we must act in fully human ways. He must use our intelligence and we must develop it by study and reflection upon our ministry. We will need to make choices and so we must learn to make loving choices by living disciplined Christian lives. Because God respects our human nature so thoroughly, we can—in the short run, not the long run—frustrate God's work by not being a well prepared living instrument even as a piano can frustrate a musician by being out of tune. And so although it is true that the healing comes totally from God, it is equally true that unless we do our part the healing will not happen. God could act differently: he could heal directly without any ministry on our part. But he has chosen to use us because we are members of Christ's body and all that he does is now done through Christ.

Religious Healing as a Process

Healing is a process. Let me illustrate what I mean by a story. Recently a friend's three year old son, Angelo, had a rash on his body. My friend decided it needed a physician's attention and so she prepared Angelo for a visit to the doctor, explaining how the doctor would make it well. The physician did the usual thing of examining the rash, made a mental diagnosis, wrote a prescription with directions for its use, and gave it to the mother. He then told the little boy that he could put his clothes back on and indicated that the visit was over.

As the doctor started to leave the room Angelo looked down at the rash and called out, "Doctor, the bumps are still there!" The doctor came back in the room, sat down and explained that the boy's mother would have to go to the drugstore and buy the medicine; then she would rub it on his "bumps" three times a day for three days and the "bumps" would gradually go away. This satisfied Angelo. He had been thinking of healing in a magical/miraculous way, but he understood that healing is a process once the physician explained it.

Prayer can affect the process in several ways. Prayer may bring healing without the use of medicine or surgery. Or it may speed up the process of healing, even to the point where it appears to be instantaneous. It may also lesson the side-effects of a medication, such as the nausea that results from chemotherapy treatment of cancer. Or it may strengthen the effects of a medication or treatment beyond what would normally be expected.

In Fr. Anthony's case prayer enabled him to withdraw from an addictive pain medication without experiencing the expected withdrawal symptoms. It also lessened his pain so that he did not need pain medication. With Fr. Anthony this lessening of pain was permanent: sometimes it is only temporary.

One needs to be cautious about praying for the cessation of pain. Pain is a signal that something is wrong and needs attention, and it is not good to turn off that signal before the proper attention is given it. If someone is having severe chest pains and it is not yet clear whether it is a heart attack or indigestion, it would be unwise to pray for a cessation of pain until a diagnosis has been made. On the other hand it was perfectly appropriate to pray for cessation of pain for Fr. Anthony who had been diagnosed and was under a physician's care.

The Healing of Fr. Anthony

The text for my homily at Fr. Anthony's funeral was:

> "In the eyes of the unwise, they did appear to die, their going looked like a disaster, their leaving us, like an annihilation; but they are in peace" (Wis 3:2–3).

I opened the homily with the following paragraph:

> "If ever a death looked like a disaster Fr. Anthony's did. He did not want to die. He struggled against death with all his

might. He was young; he had much to give; he had ministry to
do; family, community, friends to love. His illness was long
and painful. He died hollow-eyed and gaunt. Where is the
victory?"

I will not repeat the rest of the homily here: it would be
tedious and I have deepened my understanding of our ministry
since then. The homily's opening statement highlighted the fact
that our ministry was not entirely successful. But, in fact,
through the ministry of the healing team Fr. Anthony did receive
healing in all four dimensions of his being. Although the physical
healing was restricted to freedom from pain and from the stupefying medication the healing was not inconsequential. Indeed it
gave him the freedom to grow in all the other dimensions of his
life, especially in his relationship with God. In the emotional dimension the reconstruction of childhood experiences freed him
from patterns of emotional response to life situations that had
hindered his spiritual journey. This inner healing enabled him to
overcome his fear of dying and prevented the apathy that so often
dominates the seriously ill. Fr. Anthony's refusal to be mastered
by pain, fear, and discouragement was a significant victory.

Fr. Anthony received healing of his spiritual wounds. He was
healed of his distorted notion of God as distant and uncaring and
came to a new understanding of God as a caring, compassionate
Parent. This opened the way for him to make new choices. He
chose not to become a *victim* of cancer or of death. He refused to
be *just* a dying patient. He refused to become depersonalized by
his illness. Rather he became more of a person during his struggle. He came to know who he was as a son of God, and the
meaning of his life. His visitors were surprised at the energy they
felt flowing from him. One frequent visitor told me, "I always left
Tony's room feeling better than when I entered. He gave me a lot
more than I gave him."

I think the greatest healing was in his relationships. Fr. Anthony refused to become alienated from God. He refused to allow
feelings of despair to destroy his friendship with God. He strug-
gled with them and came to know God more intimately.

Fr. Anthony refused to become isolated, to be hidden away.

He chose to live his last few months with his religious community rather than in the hospital. He maintained his interest in community affairs, his family, and friends. With his refusal to be *just* a dying patient, he understood that the Lord had work for him to do even while he was sick, and he did it. He was reconciled with his brother; he provided for a continuing relationship with his sister's children, and for a handing over of his administrative duties. And for all of us, his friends, he gave a Christian witness. He showed that it was possible to be a victor over death. He pioneered the way. Each of us knows now what it means to be a traveler on the road to God's own wholeness.

8.

Healing Emotional Ills

I still have a very clear memory of an event that happened when I was three years old. It was a pleasant summer day in Ohio. My parents had decided to go for a drive into the countryside and we had stopped at a village park for a picnic lunch. My mother was spreading a blanket and setting out the food; my father was walking down the street to get some needed item from the village store. I was exploring the park some distance from my mother. Suddenly a pack of ferocious dogs attacked me, knocked me down, and, with saliva drooling from wide open mouths, were about to devour me. I screamed with terror and my mother rescued me. She tried to calm me but I would not be comforted because the dogs continued to hang around, barking and jumping, trying to get me. I can remember how utterly terrified I was of these ferocious animals. My father, hearing my screams, hurriedly returned. He sized up the situation and took me in his arms and into the car, shutting the door against these terrifying animals. He asked me to tell him what had happened. Still sobbing, I told him the story of my near destruction.

He said, "Now I will tell you a story."

"When I was a little boy, our neighbor, Mr. Foraker had a dog named Queenie. One day Mr. Foraker said he had something to show me. He took me into his garage and there was Queenie with six newborn puppies. I was so excited and I wanted to pick them up, but Mr. Foraker said they were too little now but in a few weeks I could play with them. I could hardly wait and asked Mr. Foraker almost every day if they were big enough yet. Finally one day he said they were and he brought all six of them out into the yard. I lay down and they climbed all over me, licking my face and biting my fingers and toes. I laughed and laughed and rolled over and over and they just kept licking and biting and jumping all over me. It was such fun. Mr. Foraker would let me play with them every day until they got big and then he gave them away. I was so sad: I missed them so much."

I had stopped crying by now. My father continued,

"The dogs that frightened you were puppies like Queenie's, only bigger. They wanted to play with you; they wanted to roll on the ground with you and to lick your face and bite your toes. But they were too big and you were too little."

I knew my father was the smartest man in the whole world, but he must surely be wrong this time. Those dogs didn't want to play; they wanted to kill me. I was convinced of that.

My father, reading my looks, said,

"I want you to play a pretend game with me. I want you to pretend those dogs are here again, that they have knocked you down and are standing over you—only this time I am with you, not down the road like I was before. I will protect you. Now I want you to pretend that you are very big. Reach out and take one of the dogs and start to pet it; now scratch its stomach. Now pull its tail, but don't hurt it, and watch it try to bite your hand. Are you pretending?

I answered in a scared voice, "Yes, Daddy."

My father then asked me, "What's happening?"

I told him that the dog I was petting didn't look as big as it did before and that it was licking my hand. My father then said that I could quit pretending. I quit and he and I talked about pretend games for a few minutes.

My father then said a terrifying thing. "Let's go find the dogs and play with them for real. Only this time I will be with you to protect you." I was very nervous and scared but I went along with him hesitantly. We found the dogs and I tried to be brave, but I was scared. My father didn't let them knock me over this time and he held me as I gingerly patted one of the dogs while he held the others off. I didn't enjoy it very much but it did seem that it might be fun if the dog were smaller and if there were only one of them. I told him this and the next day he brought home a tiny puppy to be my very own dog. I named her Queenie and had her as a friend for many years.

My father had done for me what Robert L. Wise in his excellent book, *Healing of the Past,* calls "The Reconstruction of Experience." He prefers this term to the more familiar terms "Healing of Memories" and "Inner Healing." He says that our emotional ills can be understood in this way: an experience that wounded me in the past, especially in early childhood, still affects my behavior just as it did at the time it happened, even though I now "know better." Even though I have forgotten the event with my conscious mind, it still resides in my unconscious memory and it still influences my behavior. This constant and irrational repetition of past behavior is the emotional wound that needs healing. Until it is healed the wounded person is not free to respond as he would like and knows he should. He is in bondage to the earlier wounding experience. But the wound can be healed by bringing it into conscious memory, reliving it now in the light of Christ's healing presence so that the original event is reconstructed. This means that it will be perceived differently, have a different meaning for the supplicant, and have a different outcome.

Although Wise calls this an "explanation" he says clearly that it still remains a mystery because it is the work of the Holy Spirit making Jesus present to the supplicant healing his emotional wounds. The "explanation" helps me know more about how healing prayer works, but ultimately it remains in the realm of faith. However this partial understanding is valuable. It takes away the "spookiness" that many people feel when they first hear of this ministry, and makes the ministers more effective in ministering healing to emotional hurts.

If my father had not healed my experience of being "attacked by a pack of ferocious dogs" I would have grown up with an unreasonable and exaggerated fear of dogs—even of harmless playful puppies.

I want to contrast what my father did for me with the prayer team's ministry to Larry described in chapter 3 for purposes of understanding what is involved in this form of ministry. For although my father did not think of what he was doing to help me cope with this traumatic event as ministry, and although he did not invoke the presence of Jesus or make use of prayer, it was healing of an emotional hurt using natural means and had many similarities to the ministry of healing emotional hurts. I will recap the healing team's ministry to Larry. Larry was severely handicapped by his feelings that he could never measure up to anyone's expectations of him. This grew out of his childhood experience of being ridiculed by his father for not measuring up. This experience was crystalized in the memory of bringing home a report card with a failing grade in English composition. Larry's father made him wear a dunce cap at the dinner table and called Larry the "family dummy." His brothers and sisters further ridiculed Larry by calling him "Dummy."

As the team reported their ministry with Larry, even before they asked him to relive this memory in his imagination, Larry spontaneously experienced God affirming his gifts and approving of him as a well loved son. This was a deeply moving experience for Larry and set the stage for the next phase of healing.

The team then instructed Larry to remember the humiliating scene at the dinner table and then to invite Jesus into the scene. Larry reported that with Jesus present in the remembered scene the entire event took a different turn than it had in the original occurrence. In the reconstruction of the event Jesus came to the table, removed the dunce cap from Larry and comforted him as he was crying. Jesus talked to him about the trouble he was having with English composition and then asked one of Larry's older sisters to help him with his homework. Jesus then talked to Larry's father about his own childhood hurts that made him be so cruel to his son. The father received healing in this scene and Larry was able to understand and forgive his father. Jesus reminded the entire family that they were all part of God's family, and as they grasped this they were able to love and support one another. The family, in the reenacted scene, experienced profound reconciliation. This is, of course, only a summary of a powerful experience that took several sessions.

I want now to note some of the similarities of what my father did for me with the ministry to Larry. In getting me to tell him what had happened he helped me relive the wounding experience. It was, of course, fresh in my mind because it had just happened. In ministry the supplicant may have "forgotten" the event and may need considerable help from the team to recall it. Prayer is often a help in his effort to recall what is at the root of his troubling symptoms. In the context of prayer the team helps the supplicant relive the wounding experience by asking her to bring it to memory and to remember it as vividly and as graphically as she possibly can. If the wounding has been the result of repeated events, such as a parent constantly belittling a child as Larry's dad did, it is well to get the supplicant to sum up the problem in a single specific event such as Larry's remembering when his father made him wear a dunce cap at the dinner table.

The next step in the reconstruction of the wounding event is to develop a new understanding of the event and some new options of how to respond to the event. My father's story of playing with Queenie's puppies stirred my imagination and I could vicariously live it out as he told it. This gave me a new understanding of dogs and their behavior, and a new way of relating to them. He could have simply told me that the dogs were not ferocious but only playful puppies, but he was wise enough to know that would not do the job. My perceptions had to be changed, but just telling me was not enough to change my perceptions. Many times in ministry we may be tempted to "explain" things to a supplicant— to tell him he has not perceived a situation correctly. Sometimes new knowledge is helpful as we see in the ministry of instruction, but to change a deeply held perception of an experience that is influencing one's behavior by merely telling the person that the perception is incorrect is not enough. The key to changing behavior is in changing the images that motivate one to act. In our ordinary language we say that we are "thinking about doing something." This is shorthand for a very complex mental process that includes the use of images, although we are seldom aware of the images. To do the simplest thing, for example sitting down, I must first have an image in my mind of this act—of the chair that I will sit on, of the various bodily movements involved in sitting down. When a young woman is taught in charm school how to walk more elegantly, she is given a new set of images through watching others and practicing what she sees.

My father's story started the process of changing my experience. He gave me another set of images: dogs knocked you down and licked your face and bit your toes for reason other than to eat you. This is puppies' way of playing. His story also gave me an alternative set of images about how I could react to the dogs' behavior. I could respond by playing and enjoyment. I hadn't been exposed to dogs and didn't know this.

In ministry God plays a significant part in supplying the supplicant with these new images. God gives the supplicant new images through a variety of means: by reading Scripture, discussion, the ministry of instruction, through prophecy or a word of knowledge. Sometimes he gives them directly to the supplicant. An example of this was when Larry spontaneously "heard" God approve of him. Sometimes God gives them to the supplicant through the healing team as for example in Larry's case one of the healing team, Peter, received an image of god as Grandfather holding Larry, as a child, on his lap and rejoicing in him as only a grandparent can. Peter shared this image with Larry so that it became part of Larry's changed perception of God as benevolent and of himself as a well loved child of God.

When my father did a reconstruction of my experience, he used the phrase "pretend game" because I was too little to understand "I want you to imagine" or "visualize what happened." But into my imaginary replay of the original terrifying event he now introduced his own presence, so that I would feel safe enough to try something new even though it would be scary. He encouraged me to try out, in my imagination, and with him present, my new perception of these dogs' behavior and a new way of relating to them, namely by "pretending" to play with one of them and to have fun rather than react in terror. With my father's help I was able to perceive the dogs as playful rather than ferocious, and I was able, in my imagination, to "pretend" that I was responding to the puppy playfully, although tentatively and timidly.

In ministry the team does something similar. Its physical presence to the supplicant while she is reliving the wounding experience gives her the support needed to relive the traumatic experience. But the team does something more that my father did not do. Into the imaginary replay of the traumatic event with the new perceptions the team introduces the presence of Jesus (or sometimes God as Parent) being present to the supplicant as she relives the original event in a new way and with a different outcome. The presence of Jesus (or of God as Parent) does far more than make the supplicant feel safe, as my father's presence did for me. Jesus' presence will do far more than any mere human presence could. Through Jesus, God's grace is brought into the reliving of the situation. Jesus indeed "rewrites the history of one's life." The facts of the original event remain the same. In the imaginative replay Larry's father still made him wear a dunce cap at the dinner table, but the presence of Jesus changes the outcome and meaning of the original event. In the relived experience Jesus removes the dunce cap, consoles the humiliated Larry, and finds a way to help him with his difficulty in school work. Jesus helps Larry see that his father's cruelty comes from his own emotional wounds. And just as the original experience of the event shaped his behavior in that he felt dumb, the new experience which the presence of Christ gives will shape his behavior. Larry no longer will think of himself as dumb and worthless. He is a child of God, well loved by him and gifted by him, approved of by him. This is what Wise means by "reconstruction of the experience."

Healing of Emotional Ills Is a Process

This "rewriting of one's history" is a process that takes time. This is so for several reasons. First, usually there have been many hurtful events, with many people involved, that have contributed to the supplicant's wounded emotional life. To "rewrite" all of this history will take many sessions of bringing Christ's presence to bear on each important event and person.

Second, even if Jesus has dramatically healed the supplicant's wounded emotions this inner healing needs to work itself out into external behavior. Just as my father, after the pretend game, had me find the real dogs and play with them and finally got a dog for me, so in ministry the healing is a process that works from the inside out. The phrase "healing an emotional wound" is deceptive: it makes the healing sound too simple. If I should cut my finger—even severely—and should God heal it dramatically, there is little I would have to change in external behavior. The wound did not cause me to behave differently than before in any significant way, and so the healing of the physical wound does not entail a change in external behavior. But with Larry, for example, years of ridicule had so damaged his self-image that it significantly affected his behavior. He thought of himself as incompetent and so he behaved incompetently. After being healed of this damaged self-image as one who could not measure up, he now had to learn how to behave as a well loved child of God who had given him many talents. Larry needed time and help from others to make this change in behavior. It takes time to break old habitual patterns and to discover, and learn to use, unrecognized talents. Thus the need for follow-up ministry.

The team may be the ones to help the person integrate her new self-image into her total way of life, but it may be that someone else who is giving overall pastoral care would be the person to do this, or a spiritual director, or a spiritual companion, or a counselor.

But there is still another need frequently after healing of an emotional wound. Almost certainly this healing will have implications in the supplicant's spiritual life. The person is now freer to grow spiritually than before and he may need help in doing so. He may need some guidance about his spiritual life, discipline, reading Scripture, praying, carrying out his duties in life, relating to people in new ways.

9.

More on Healing Spiritual Wounds

Sally, sitting opposite me in my office, was bent over double in her chair with emotional pain. Between sobs, she said, "I wish I'd never been born: I feel so totally empty and my life has no meaning." This was our initial visit. After a few minutes she was able to tell me more about herself and why she had asked to see me.

Sally was then thirty-five, had been married briefly in her twenties, and was divorced with no children. She had done graduate work in a prestigious Ivy League university, but had not finished work for her degree. She had grown up in a troubled home: her parents had been inadequate to the task of raising children, so she and her sister had suffered considerable neglect. Both of her parents had come from strict religious families but had dropped all religious practice, so their children had received no religious training. Her only knowledge of religion came from two college courses: the comparative study of religions and the Bible as literature.

Recently Sally had expressed a personal interest in religion to an acquaintance who took her to a charismatic prayer meeting. After the meeting she went to the prayer ministry room. She told the praying team about the terrible emptiness she felt. They prayed for healing of her childhood experience of parental neglect. She went back next week and told them that nothing had happened. They then told her that she needed to make a decision for Christ. This frightened her and she left, worried and upset. Her friend suggested that Sally call me and ask if I would talk to her, which I agreed to do.

Although Sally had a superior mind and many talents, when she first visited me she was working in a restaurant as a dishwasher. Sally's studies in graduate school had been in ancient semitic languages and she had worked for a famous scholar as a research assistant for several years. She could easily have gotten work in this field even without her degree. But she said that she no longer cared; she worked only to support herself minimally.

She told me that her interest in religion came from a hope that it would fill the terrible emptiness she always felt and would take away her meaningless existence. But as we talked I discovered that for Sally God was a dangerous person. She was so frightened of him that she couldn't pray or do religious things. The very thought of letting him have any control of her life terrified her. This explained to me why she had been so frightened by the prayer team's attempt to get her to commit her life to Christ.

Sally's intelligence was a great help in our work together. She was introspective and able to see herself realistically. She said, "I know that I am intelligent and have talents but I can't really believe that I can do anything worthwhile. I drive myself at tasks I take on but I get no enjoyment from my work. It seems worthless."

When we discussed her failed marriage she said, "The central problem was love. I can't experience love. I feel I am unlovable and I find it imposible to love anyone else. Sexual intimacy is frightening to me."

Further discussion surfaced other problems. She was indifferent about her physical appearance, and would not get medical attention when she needed it. She hoarded food and ate compulsively without enjoyment.

My assessment of Sally was that although she had many emotional wounds that needed healing, her primary wounds were spiritual. If my assessment was correct, emotional healing would not be effective until her spiritual wounds were healed. Her distorted idea of God as a terrifying person, her inability to experience love, her feelings of absolute emptiness and meaningless were symptoms that pointed to spiritual woundedness. I discussed my assessment with Sally and suggested that my ministry would focus on spiritual growth as well as healing of spiritual wounds. Sally responded quite favorably to this proposal. We agreed to spend some time working with her spirituality.

Sally's experience with the prayer team illustrates the diffi-culty supplicants have in getting ministry for their spiritual needs. On Sally's second visit the prayer room ministers recog-nized her spiritual need and made a clumsy attempt to meet it by asking her to make a decision for Christ—the very thing she was least able to do. Their clumsiness is understandable. Until re-cently the field of spirituality has been largely restricted to the clergy. So the laity have not been trained to minister to spiritual needs. But this needs to change. Prayer teams need to be trained to minister to spiritual woundedness. At the very least there is a certain degree of spiritual woundedness involved in every other kind of woundedness.

But there is such a thing as a spiritual illness—a hurt in its own right which is the primary cause of various symptoms. Se-vere forms, as in Sally's case, are often characterized by hopeless-ness, a lack of meaning to one's life, absolute emptiness and extreme loneliness. A spiritual wound may be at the bottom of other hurts—physical, as physicians are recognizing, emotional, and relational disturbances which will not be healed until the spiritual wound is healed—as I judged to be the case with Sally.

Admittedly in assessing the supplicant's needs it is difficult to distinguish between emotional healing and spiritual wound-edness because both use the same channels—intellect, will and emotions—to express their symptoms. Nevertheless the spiritual dimension is different from the emotional and deserves attention in its own right. But not every spiritual need of a supplicant can be met by healing prayer. There is a difference between growth, maintenance and healing in the spiritual life just as there is in physical life.

• **Growth:**   In the physical order a newborn child needs the proper food, nurturing care and mothering in order to develop in a systematic and predictable way in order to become a fully adult human being.

So, too, in the spiritual order a person needs instruction about God, and a faith community that provides needed experience if he is to become a mature Christian.

- **Maintenance:** Once a person has become a mature adult in the physical order, he still needs a proper diet and exercise to maintain his healthy development.

    So, too, in the spiritual order a mature Christian must continue to be nourished on God's word and the sacraments and have a faith community to maintain his spiritual development.

- **Healing:** In the physical order a broken bone needs to be set, placed in a cast and cared for in order to be healed.

    In our spiritual lives traumatic experiences and/or deprivations can so wound us that we cannot respond adequately to God's call to share in his divine nature. Spiritual remedies are needed to heal spiritual wounds.

It is common to find that a supplicant who needs spiritual healing also needs help with spiritual growth as well. This was true of Sally. She had hardly started her spiritual journey.

Christian Spirituality

"Everyone who does what is right has been begotten by God. See how much the Father has loved us! His love is so great that we are called God's children—and so in fact we are" (1 Jn 2:29—3:1).

I have quoted John to counteract a mentality that restricts the use of "spirituality" to doing holy things like saying prayers and reading the Bible. John tells us that God our Father has called us, through Christ, to become members of his family. As adopted children we are to share in his divine nature. Our part is to respond, with the help of the Holy Spirit, to this call. As John puts it, we are to do what is right. That is to say, we are to live the divine life as seen in Jesus. Our response comes from our total being. Every dimension of our being is involved. Every thought, desire and action make up our response. Our spirituality is the totality of our life. Nothing of our life is not part of our spirituality. Our spirituality is the steps we take to actualize our divine nature in our daily life. Spiritually, we can be more or less healthy. We are spiritually healthy when we are doing all that we can, under God's grace, to respond to God's call. We are spiritually ill to the degree that our response to God's loving call is inadequate. Spiritual wounds (or hurts) are those things which prevent us from making an adequate response. This spiritual woundednes can be located in our mind by not being in conformity with the mind of Christ, or in our will when our will is not in conformity with the will of the Father. Spiritual healing brings our minds into conformity with Christ's and our wills into conformity with God's plan for us. Only then can we adequately respond to God's loving call to share in his divine nature.

Spiritual Ills Related to the Mind

There are a number of ways in which our minds are not in conformity with the mind of Christ.

- **Lack of Information:** A common spiritual ill related to the mind is lack of information. Sally could not respond to God's call because she had no experience of God as a loving Parent because she had not been taught about God as a child. Many of us suffer from this ill in a lesser way. We can have "head" knowledge and still lack "heart" knowledge. We can quote John 3:16, "God loved the world so much that he gave his only Son, so that everyone who believes in him may not die but have eternal life," but still find it difficult to believe that God loves *me*.

- **Distorted Information:** Another common spiritual ill related to the mind is to have distorted information. For example Sally thought of God as someone "out to get her." God, for her, was a dangerous and terrifying person. Many of us suffer from this kind of spiritual ill in a lesser way. For example, a very common distortion in Roman Catholic circles is that God sends sickness to us.

• **Worldly Values:** Another spiritual ill that nearly all of us suffer from is having adopted attitudes and values from the worldly culture we live in. For example, our culture teaches us to place our security in money and possessions in a way that makes it difficult to trust in God's care for his children.

• **Distorted Self-Image:** A very common spiritual wound among those asking for healing prayer is a distorted image of themselves. Sally was wounded in this way. She was not able to use her superior intelligence and other abilities because she thought she didn't amount to anything and couldn't really do anything significant. It was as if she had a tape recorder running in her head constantly repeating "You will never amount to anything; your parents were weird; you're weird; you can't do anything right."

Spiritual Ills Related to the Will

Our will can be hurt in some way so that we are not able to make the kind of choices that allow us to respond adequately to God's loving call.

- **Compulsive Behavior:** Compulsive behavior is a spiritual wound that troubles many supplicants. In spite of sincere and prolonged struggles, even using spiritual resources, they are not free to make choices in the area of alcohol, drugs, sex, and food. They are compelled to use them in destructive ways. (Please note that I am not saying that every such wrong use of them is due to a compulsion.) Sally's use of food was compulsive.

- **Inability To Love:** A very serious spiritual wound related to the will is the inability or unwillingness to love. Sally spoke of this inability as being the central problem in her failed marriage. Sometimes the wound is a refusal to love. Closely associated with this is the inability or refusal to forgive. I think of a woman who professed to be a Christian but refused to even see the children of her daughter because the daughter married a man the woman disapproved of. When she came for ministry finally because of physical problems this refusal to love turned out to be the root cause of her physical problems.

Resources for Spiritual Growth and Healing

My overall plan with Sally was twofold: healing for her spiritual ills and to provide the means for spiritual growth.

Her first need was knowledge of God as a loving Parent who loved *her* personally to counteract both her ignorance of God and her distorted view of him. But I knew that theoretical knowledge would not be enough: she needed to *experience* God as loving Parent. Her second greatest need was to start learning how to respond to this loving Parent by prayer.

To meet the need for knowledge I made use of the ministry of instruction. This was a teachable moment for Sally. I arranged for her to meet weekly with Fr. Albert, a retired professor of theology, who was willing to instruct her in just those truths of the faith that she needed at this moment of her life.

To meet her need to experience God as Parent loving her I taught her how to *experience* God in praying Scripture passages. In preparation for our weekly meetings Sally would read assigned passages from the Bible: passages that would portray God in a loving and nurturing way. One such passage was Zephaniah 3:16–17:

> "Zion, have no fear,
> do not let your hands fall limp.
> Yawheh your God is in your midst,
> a victorious warrior.
> He will exult with joy over you,
> he will renew you by his love;
> he will dance with shouts of joy for you
> as on a day of festival."

When we met we would discuss her reaction to the passage or questions she had about their meaning. Then I would read one of them to her, inserting her name in place of Zion, or Daughter, to make it more personal. We would spend some time in silence and then I would ask her what she was experiencing, and we would discuss that. Gradually she came to experience God as a loving and caring Parent who loved her personally.

After I had taught her this method of praying Scripture she continued it on her own and would often comment on the power of Scripture to transform her life.

Her intelligence was an asset in her work with Fr. Albert. He enjoyed the challenge of a bright pupil who was an eager student. She quickly learned a great deal of Christian theology.

As she progressed in the spiritual life, I taught her to meditate on the life of Jesus and to use the prayer of praise—especially in times of discouragement and difficulty.

After she was feeling more comfortable with God, I arranged for her to have weekly sessions with a healing team. They prayed for healing of her wounded emotional life stemming from her early childhood experiences, her terror of God, and to silence the "tapes running in her head" that said she couldn't do anything worthwhile. Sally reported that their ministry was effective. She especially valued their use of blessed oil and laying on of hands. But the best thing they did for Sally was a generous use of the prayer of affirmation. As a result of their ministry she resumed her graduate studies and eventually became a recognized scholar in the area of biblical languages.

After about six months she decided to become a Christian. In preparation for this she made use of the healing team to help her forgive her parents for their lack of care for her. This was quite hard for her to do. They had her make daily use of the aspiration "Lord Jesus, I place my parents in the cathedral of your heart." While praying this way she, in her imagination, saw her parents being received by Jesus, embracing them and loving them. Then Jesus called her into the scene and told her that she had failed in love, too, since she was harboring bitterness toward them for their failures. He then asked her to forgive them and to repent of her bitterness and lack of love, and to ask their forgiveness. In the scene she did so and they embraced. In real life she re-established a relationship with her parents from whom whe had been estranged. This later turned out to be a healing of her inability to love others.

At an Easter vigil liturgy she was baptized, confirmed and received First Eucharist. This was a major turning point in her life. The liturgy of baptism gave her a sense of a new beginning, and of belonging to a community of people. Several years later she told me, "I still have a lot of emotional pain, but after baptism I have never felt that terrible emptiness and meaninglessness of my life. I now know that I have a destiny." She received Holy Communion frequently and found it to be a healing sacrament. When receiving Communion she would ask Jesus to heal some part of her that still seemed to be wounded and she experienced him touching and healing her inner being.

Follow-Up Ministry

Several weeks after her baptism Sally said she now felt well enough that she wanted to discontinue formal ministry. I agreed that she was ready to discontinue weekly ministry, but told her that I thought follow-up ministry was essential. Her spiritual wounds had been healed but there was now need to maintain the healing and to grow in her spiritual life. But there was another reason: the healing that has taken place in her inner being must now percolate out into her external way of life and this takes time and usually the help of others.

I was soon to move to a new assignment, so I could not do follow-up ministry. However, Fr. Albert was delighted to offer this ministry to her. He would see her once a month and be available if she was having a difficult time. Sally kept in touch with me through an occasional letter and mutual friends.

An important element of follow-up ministry is being part of a stable faith community that possesses the resources needed for both maintenance and growth. This usually means being a member of a parish or congregation. The healed supplicant needs to live in a context of faith, hope, and love. He needs the inspiration provided by fellow Christians attempting to be faithful followers of Christ. So Fr. Albert helped Sally become an active member of the parish in which she had been baptized. In addition to the community of faith in the parish, Fr. Albert encouraged Sally to make a cursillo and to become active in that movement. This gave her a smaller and more intimate group with which to share her life. It also met another need: that of regular accountability. Being accountable to another or to a group is a powerful way to help the inner healing percolate out into one's everyday behavior.

Sometimes the follow-up takes the form of an opportunity for offering a meaningful Christian service. After a year of follow-up ministry, Fr. Albert raised this issue with Sally. She decided to do volunteer work with children severely retarded developmentally.

Fr. Albert monitored Sally's prayer life and taught her new

ways of praying at the proper time so that she would continue to progress in her ability to pray. After about a year with Fr. Albert, Sally had to move to a new location and felt that she was able to continue to live her spiritual life without any special help. She continues to be serious about her spiritual journey and is living a happy and productive Christian life.

The ministry of spiritual healing is awesome. Paul himself found it so. He says, "All this is done by God, who through Christ changed us from enemies into his friends, and gave us the task of making others his friends also" (2 Cor 5:18–19). So, confronted with exercising this ministry, we say, "Who am I to make someone else a friend of God?" Yet each one of us has been called to this ministry to some degree. We need to discern to what degree we are called and for whom. It is a demanding, but rewarding ministry. It teaches us more about the transforming power of God's love than anything else we can do.

10.

Prayer for Healing Wounded Relationships

"Father, I've never been so hurt in my entire life."

Ida started to sob. I pushed the box of tissues across my desk close to her and waited for her to regain her composure. I had known Ida a long time. She was a widow in her early sixties. She and her lifelong friend, Vivian, also a widow, had decided to share a house together and had been living together several months. Ida continued her story.

> "Yesterday Vivian blew up at me. I was sitting in the front room reading. Vivian was running the sweeper. All of a sudden she stopped and shouted at me, 'You lazy slob! I wish to hell that I'd never met you. All you do is sit around the house and expect me to clean up after you.' I was shocked and started to cry. Then I got mad and told her that I was sick and tired of her always fussing around moving my things around and sticking them in drawers so I couldn't find them. I called her a 'fussy old mother hen.' I'm so mad at her . . . But I don't want to hate her the way I do right now. We've been good friends since we were kids, and I don't want to lose this friendship. I can't afford to; I haven't got many friends left anymore. Father, can you help me straighten out this mess?"

Relationships are not optional for human beings. From birth to death we are dependent upon others for our very existence. Without satisfying and nurturing relationships we can become sick and may even die. It is not unknown for the surviving spouse to lose the will to live and to die soon after the death of a marriage partner. Important relationships are vital to our well-being.

But, like Ida, we sometimes manage our most important relationships badly: those with our parents, children, spouses, friends, working partners. Then these important relationships become a destructive force in our lives, causing us hurts that need healing. This is what Ida was asking for.

Sometimes the person with wounded relationships will seek help from a prayer team as Ida did. A knowledge of the many sources of hurt in a relationship will aid the team in devising a plan of action to bring healing to the wounded relationship. So I want now to talk about some of the more common sources of hurt.

Sources of Hurt in Relationships

Violation of Explicit Agreements

During their engagement a young couple decided that they would have children soon after marriage and the wife would quit working. However, after the first child was born, the husband decided to return to college. This necessitated the wife's going back to work and placing the child in day care. The woman was not in agreement with this plan and felt that the husband had gone back on his agreement and was very hurt. Their relationship rapidly deteriorated.

Violation of Unexpressed Expectations

Our expectations of another are frequently unexpressed and sometimes we are even unaware of them ourselves. We form these expectations early in life by adopting the attitudes of people important to us, such as parents. In an unthinking way we come to believe that their way of relating to others is the only right way. These unconscious expectations have great power over our behavior. They have the quality of "You *must* meet my expectation." Let me illustrate what I mean.

A recently married woman came for ministry very upset with

her husband. In discussing her problem she reported that although her husband was very loving, generally thoughtful, and helpful in many ways, he absolutely refused to do any work in the kitchen. He would not even fix a snack or make coffee for himself but expected her to do it for him. She resented this, saying that he expected her to be his slave. He on the other hand insisted that this was woman's work.

In looking at their early family experiences it turned out that the husband came from a rural family that sharply divided the roles of men and women. His father and mother, and both sets of grandparents, believed that preparing food was women's work. The husband could not even conceive of any other arrangement. The wife on the other hand had come from an urban family in which both parents shared equally in all the household tasks, including food preparation. She too could not even conceive of any other arrangement. Both felt that the other had violated an agreement, but it was only an unexpressed expectation that each had of the other. They had not discussed it before marriage.

Conflicts and Quarrels

People in relationships have different needs and desires and these sometimes clash. Conflict in itself is not hurtful. It can lead to maturity and to growth in a relationship. But sometimes the parties cannot find a constructive way of resolving the conflict and end up quarreling and blaming the other as Vivian and Ida did.

When Ida was able to discuss the quarrel more calmly it became apparent that literature and needlework were important to her and that she spent a great deal of time with both. The appearance of the house was not very important to her, and never had been even in her former home.

On the other hand Vivian's greatest interest was a beautiful home and she cheerfully spent a lot of time cleaning and decorating. But she resented Ida's lack of cooperation in housekeeping. Only dimly aware of these different desires, they had not even attempted to reach a mutually agreeable resolution to this conflict of interests and had ended up in an angry name-calling session.

Immature Relationships

A husband seeking ministry said that he is baffled with his wife's jealous behavior and wants help. He reports an incident typical of his wife's relationship to him. They were dining with another couple in a restaurant. While taking their orders the waitress—previously unknown to any of them—said to him "my dear." His wife stood up and angrily shouted at the waitress, "He is not 'your dear'; he's 'my dear' and don't you forget it." He and the other couple were terribly embarrassed at this jealous outburst. He asks the team, "Will prayer help?"

Immaturity or inner woundedness can cause us to act destructively in our important relationships, such as husband-wife, parent-child, friendships, and even in relationships with institutions such as the Church. The destructiveness takes many forms such as excessive dependency upon the other, dominating the other, physical and sexual abuse, jealousy, and possessiveness.

Intentional Hurts

Perhaps the most painful wounds, and the most difficult to heal, are those resulting from intentional cruelty. When I was chaplain in a hospital I visited an elderly lady who had been badly beaten by a young man who had broken into her apartment to rob her. She was not physically capable of preventing the robbery. The intruder had beaten her for no reason except sadistic pleasure. She said, "I can forgive him for robbing me. I know what it is to need money. But I find it hard to forgive his deliberate cruelty." This example of intentional cruelty is extreme, but the deliberate use of cruel remarks, racial slurs, and put-downs are common even among family and friends.

Unintentional Hurts

Even unintentional events can seriously wound relationships. I remember a tragic accident in my childhood that disrupted our neighborhood. During a game of "cops and robbers" John, age ten, was shot and killed by a playmate, Harold, who thought the gun he was playing with was empty. Everyone knew it was unintentional, but John's parents blamed Harold's parents and were unwilling to forgive either Harold or his parents. We kids were confused. We did not know how to relate to Harold and mostly avoided him. Out of hurt, Harold's family eventually moved away from the neighborhood with the relationships unhealed. Could prayer ministry have helped in this situation?

Healing Wounded Relationships

Occasionally both parties to a wounded relationship—husband and wife, parents and child, friend and friend, even entire families—will ask for ministry from a prayer team. It is possible to minister to them as a unit but the more common arrangement is to minister to them individually. Most often, however, only one of the parties asks for help. In the following discussion I have in mind ministering to an individual rather than to a group.

Healing a wounded relationship will almost always involve emotional and spiritual healing, and so what was said about them earlier in the book is applicable here. But there are some special considerations in relational healing. For example, the ministry may reveal the supplicant's need to change his expectations of the other, or to give up his own viewpoint as the only way to look at things and accept the other's as equally valid. Or the supplicant may need to look honestly at his own immaturity and do some growing up. This might mean making use of a psychological or spiritual counselor.

The team should keep two elements in mind as they minister relational healing. This ministry provides the supplicant with a unique opportunity to discover, and repent of, personal sin in his own way of relating to others. It also exposes the supplicant's need to forgive others or seek their forgiveness.

Steps in Healing a Wounded Relationship

The first step in healing a wounded relationship is for the team to help the supplicant affirm (or reaffirm) that Jesus is Lord of her life. This is best done in the form of a prayer in which the supplicant invites Jesus to be Lord of her life here and now.

Such a declaration is not always easy to make. To honestly reaffirm her earlier decision that Jesus' way of love is to be her rule of life in the face of this difficult situation may test the supplicant's sincerity and precipitate some soul-searching. She may need the team's help to be able to meet this challenge for growth in her spiritual life.

It may be that the supplicant has never deliberately and consciously invited Jesus to be Lord of her life. If this is the case the supplicant may need considerable help from the team. She may need some explanation of what making Jesus Lord will mean in her daily life. The team might recommend a book and then discuss it with her. The team might recommend that the supplicant attend a Life in the Spirit seminar or make a cursillo or a retreat. This first step needs to be taken even if it means deferring prayer for healing the relationship for some time.

To ask someone to make Jesus Lord of her life when she has never considered this before is asking someone to make a very radical change in her life, and may expose much else that needs to be done before the wounded relationship can be healed. If the team thinks of its ministry solely as praying rather than of caring for the total person, it is likely to skip over this first step and start immediately to pray for healing.

Or a team inexperienced in pastoral care may find it difficult to talk to the supplicant about such intimate spiritual matters. To them it may feel like an invasion of the person's privacy and so they skip over this first step. It is a delicate pastoral task and must be handled sensitively, but it is the foundation of all else that happens in this ministry and must *not* be passed over. To neglect it may render any other prayer ministry ineffective.

The second step is for the team to help the supplicant explicitly invite Jesus to be Lord of this *relationship* that is wounded. This is best done in the form of a prayer. This may be the first time the supplicant has thought about Jesus being Lord of a *relationship* and she may need help to think through what this will mean. But even if it is a reaffirmation of something that she has affirmed before, as in a marriage, yet there will be something new about it this time: some new growth required, or a giving over of some new thing to Jesus as Lord of this relationship in *this* situation.

To help the supplicant release her hurt feelings about the other person in the wounded relationship I sometimes suggest to the supplicant the following method of prayer.

> "Bring to mind some image of the Heart of Jesus—perhaps a spacious and beautiful cathedral filled with love. And then in a relaxed and peaceful way start using the aspiration 'Jesus, I place (name) in the cathedral of your heart.' Do this in rhythm with your breathing for several minutes and attempt to bring the other person into the scene and perhaps even see or hear or feel what Jesus is doing in regard to the other person. After praying this way for a few minutes you may sense Jesus responding to you, saying something such as 'Be compassionate as I am compassionate' or 'I have given my life that (name) may have life.' "

This will lead naturally to the next step in the process of making Jesus Lord of this relationship, which is to repent of one's own part in the wounding of the relationship. It may be that the supplicant will have to give up her unrealistic and demanding expectations of the other person. Perhaps, upon reflection, she can see her immaturity expressed in possessiveness, overdependence, or jealousy. Or perhaps she has taken the other for granted and not valued him or her as a gift from God. Each of these insights are invitations from the Lord to spiritual growth, which is to say repentance. And so it is not unusual for the supplicant to start out seeking how she might forgive the other in this wounded relationship, and find that she needs to ask the other for forgiveness.

In asking for forgiveness it is best to say explicitly, "Will you forgive me for (name the offense)?" The clarity of the question lets the other person know that you want to heal the relationship and it identifies for him what you think has wounded it. It is also important for the one being asked for forgiveness to make a clear response, such as, "Yes I do forgive you," or "I need to talk this over with you first," or "I need some time to handle this but I will get back to you." When asked for forgiveness it is not helpful to brush it off by saying something such as "It wasn't anything" or "It didn't matter."

However, there are exceptions to this direct approach. Some people are not able to handle situations that are emotionally charged. Talking about forgiveness would only embarrass them further and be counterproductive, in which case some symbolic action to indicate the wish to make amends, such as a gift or card, would be better. Putting a person in a situation which she cannot handle is not a loving thing to do.

During ministry the supplicant may discover that she needs to forgive someone—even without being asked—for hurts that person has inflicted. Forgiving another is a two step process: making a decision to forgive, and letting go of the emotions of anger and hurt. The steps already mentioned in making Jesus Lord of the relationship will usually enable the supplicant to forgive the other person. But sometimes a supplicant will find it seemingly impossible to forgive. This difficulty in forgiving may indicate the need for healing of memories. The inner wounds may be so raw that they prevent forgiveness. If this is the case, once the memories are healed forgiveness will be possible.

But difficulty in forgiving may also indicate the need to give up unrealistic expectations of the other person. The supplicant will probably be unconscious of holding on to these unrealistic expectations and will need help to become aware of them— perhaps the help of a psychological counselor. An example may illustrate what I mean.

Ursula came to our prayer team seeking inner healing. She was a deeply spiritual woman, devoted to helping crippled children, and in her late forties. She told us that she was emotionally scarred from being raised in a physically violent and chaotic family. She said that she especially wanted help in getting over the anger she felt toward her mother. They quarreled whenever they talked. In spite of repeated efforts she could not forgive her mother for having been such an uncaring mother. Discussion made it clear that the mother had been mentally ill during Ursula's childhood, and in fact still was. Further discussion made it clear that the reason Ursula was not able to forgive her mother was that she held on to the expectation that her mother *should* have loved her then and *should* love her even now. This expectation had the quality of a demand. Given the mother's mental illness, this was totally unrealistic. Unconsciously Ursula was withholding her forgiveness in an attempt to force her mother to love her. With the prayer team's help Ursula was able to admit that her mother had been incapable of loving as a mother should. She was then able to let go of the unrealizable expectation and to forgive her mother for the wounds caused by being deprived of maternal love.

The team may need to instruct a supplicant having difficulty forgiving another in methods of prayer that will facilitate forgiveness. I have found that two books, *Healing Life's Hurts* by Dennis and Mathew Linn, S.J. and *Learning to Forgive* by Doris Donnelly, are especially helpful to supplicants having difficulty in forgiving. Both give a number of helpful techniques. I personally regard the prayer of praise to be useful when I find it difficult to forgive someone. I praise God for this person, or this situation, and even for the hurt of this relationship. I can do this with sincerity because of my conviction that God will bring good out of even sinful situations.

I also use the prayer of thanksgiving . I thank God for the gift that this person is to others or has been to me. I thank God for all the gifts that he has given to this person. When I am having great difficulty in forgiving I ask God to bless this person's ministry twice as much as he blesses mine. I usually find all of this hard to do in the beginning, but if I force myself to say the words I soon find that I can say them with some degree of sincerity. What started as a clenched-jaw act of will ends in a real change of heart. Over time I have observed that God does answer this prayer and has blessed the ministry of the other more than mine. I find it amazing that through a struggle to gain a forgiving heart God is glorified and the body of Christ is built up.

Some Pastoral Cautions

We live in an age of pop psychology that believes that conflicts are best settled by talking about how we feel about things. This is sometimes true but not always. Sometimes it just muddles things even more. This is especially true when neither party is healed sufficiently to be able to forgive the other. Also, as I mentioned earlier, some people are not skilled or comfortable in talking about feelings. They prefer to heal a wounded relationship by indirect means or by a symbolic action, such as giving a gift. Their intention behind this style of seeking reconciliation should be respected as genuinely loving.

Perhaps the greatest potential danger in the area of forgiveness is making the mistake of equating *forgiveness* with *restoration of the relationship*. They are *not* the same. To forgive is to once again direct our love toward a person from whom we have withdrawn it. Ideally forgiveness should lead to reestablishing the relationship to its former status. But it is not always possible or even a loving thing to do. We must always forgive, but not always restore the relationship. Much harm is done when these two things are confused. Let me illustrate.

Emma sought help from a prayer team. She had recently discovered that her husband was sexually abusing their eldest daughter. Emma and the children, on the advice of a social worker, were living apart from the father. Through the team's ministry Emma experienced considerable healing of the hurt. After much internal struggle she was finally able to let go of the bitterness she felt toward her husband and forgive him. However, the team mistakenly told her that full forgiveness included reconciliation, meaning restoration of the relationship. Even though the social worker had told her not to allow the husband alone with the daughter, Emma followed the team's instructions and returned with the children to live with her husband. Tragically the sexual abuse of the daughter was soon repeated. Restoring the relationship was not a loving act for the husband, daughter, or herself.

11.

Prayer for Healing Wounded Relationships with God

The prayer team sat in silence, stunned at the vehemence of Susan's outburst. Susan, the supplicant, was now crying in embarrassment, saying, "I shouldn't have said that."

Susan had asked for ministry from the parish prayer team. This was their first meeting. The team leader had just asked what she was seeking ministry for. Susan had responded, "I am so angry with God that I would spit in his face if I could see him." It was this statement that had shocked the team and embarrassed Susan. Further inquiry produced a story of the tragic death of Susan's husband and infant son in a house fire.

A healing team needs to be aware that supplicants frequently have negative feelings toward God. They may be angry with God, feeling that he has treated them unfairly, or they may be disappointed with him, feeling that he has let them down when they needed him most. It is especially hard for supplicants to express anger at God because they, like Susan, know that they are "not supposed to feel this way." They may also fear what the team will think of them for having such feelings. And so the team needs to routinely explore whether or not a supplicant has these feelings and then help the supplicant express them.

It may also be hard for the team members, who love and reverence God, to permit the supplicant to speak of God in such negative ways. They may be shocked, as Susan's team was, or they may rush to God's defense and rebuke the supplicant. But if the wounded relationship between the supplicant and God is to be healed the negatve feelings must be accepted by the supplicant and the team. Only then can the root problem behind the feelings be located and healed.

Although there are advantages in ministering to a wounded relationship with God in terms of a relationship, at some point the hurt will have to be ministered to as a spiritual wound. Although the immediate cause will usually be some tragedy, such as the death of a loved one, a serious illness, or a financial hardship, the more basic cause will be a combination of an immature relationship with God and unrealistic expectations of him. Let me explain what I mean.

We have been taught that God is all knowing and all powerful. But we may not have been taught that God chose to heal and bless us through accepting the limitation of God becoming human. This is the meaning of the incarnation. This is the mystery of the cross. If we have not been taught this understanding of God's way of acting in the world, we will view him as a giant puppeteer. In this view of God, every creature in the world is a puppet connected to God by a string and God manipulates each creature to bring about every event. It is this view of God and his universe that makes us say, "He has taken my loved one away from me," or "He has sent this painful illness upon me." We then feel that God is not being loving and we respond with hurt feelings toward him.

This immature understanding of God, which is really a spiritual wound, is the root cause of the wounded relationship with God and will have to be corrected before the relationship can be healed. And all the resources discussed in the chapter on healing spiritual wounds should be used.

But a wounded relationship with God also has elements of an emotional woundedness. The supplicant's relationship with God may have been wounded by some traumatic event, as it was in Susan's case. Then the team should treat it as an emotional wound and use all the resources available for emotional healing. Reconstruction of the experience by use of the imagination and letting God speak through the ministry of the team can be very healing.

In Susan's case the team had her go back, in memory, to the tragic fire that killed her husband and child. Then in prayer they brought Jesus' presence into that scene. In the scene this time Jesus held Susan and wept with her at the tragedy of a fire that killed her husband and child. After several sessions like this she was able to release her bitterness toward God and forgive him and ask for his forgiveness for thinking so badly of him. Also through instruction by the team she came to a more mature understanding of the nature of God and his relationship to his creatures.

Wounded Relationships with the Church

I was standing at the counter of the dry cleaner's in my black suit and Roman collar. The lady behind the counter asked me if I was a Lutheran minister. I said, "No. I am a Roman Catholic priest." I asked if she was Lutheran. She said, "No, I was a Catholic once. But the priest treated us so badly when grandmother died that I said 'shove it.' I'm nothing now." I told her I was sorry to hear she had been treated so badly and asked if I could be of help in resolving things. She said, "Maybe," so I gave her my card. She told me that her name was Ruby. Later she telephoned and I arranged for her to meet with our prayer team for ministry.

Ruby's story is not uncommon. Many people who come for ministry have a wounded relationship with the Church. Someone who represents the Church has done something, or failed to do something, that has caused them hurt. As they perceive it, it is not just a person who has hurt them, it is the Church. Because the Church is an institution whose structures are sometimes impersonal, they don't know how to heal and restore the wounded relationship. A prayer team representing the Church can often act in the name of the Church and bring about healing and reconciliation.

With Ruby, for example, we used the standard methods of praying for healing of emotional wounds. We had Ruby return to the painful memory of the priest being unhelpful at the time of her grandmother's death and then invoked the presence of Jesus. At one crucial point in the process of reconciliation between Ruby's family and the priest, I stood in proxy for the priest and asked Ruby to forgive me. Because I too represented the Church for her, my action enabled her to forgive the Church in forgiving me. Ruby's former relationship with the Church was restored.

MINISTRIES THAT OFTEN GO UNRECOGNIZED

Christian ministers of healing frequently forget that there are many ways of ministering to human hurts, and so restrict themselves solely to the use of prayer. In this section I will discuss four other traditional Christian ministries that can be powerful means of healing. They are:

1. Extending hospitality.
2. Comforting.
3. Accepting self-disclosure.
4. Giving instruction.

You have certainly helped others in these ways but perhaps have never thought of them as forms of ministry. Making them a part of your ministry will give you more ways to help others.

12.

Extending Hospitality

During a telephone conversation my lifelong friend, Bill, who was living in a distant city, said:

> "Leo, what's going on? You sound depressed and un-happy."
> "Well, I guess I am, Bill," I replied. "For one thing, I feel lonely. I have reached a place in my career where I am at a standstill and I need to change directions. I'm not sure what that will be yet. I'm physically worn out and feel overwhelmed."

> After a moment or two, Bill said: "It sounds as though you could use a change of scene to sort things out. Would you like to come here? Mary and the kids would be glad to see you and so would I. We haven't had a good visit for ages."

I accepted his invitation and stayed with him several weeks. I spent time playing with his children; I sometimes worked in the garden; I got extra rest and usually took a long walk each day. I found a counselor who helped me sort out the important issues and pinpoint the decisions I needed to make. I found a spiritual director who helped me to hear the Lord's call.

I did not use my friend for any of this, and when we were together, I seldom even talked about it with him. We talked about old friends; we watched TV together, and mostly just enjoyed each other's company. The counselor and spiritual director helped me make the decisions needed to put my life in order, but the hospitality of my friend and his family made this possible.

I'm sure that the idea of ministry never crossed Bill's mind. He did not lay hands on me or pray over me, but he gave me precisely what I needed and could not get anywhere else. He ministered hospitality to me. He made space for me in his home, family and heart. Through Bill and his family I received the peace of Christ that carried me forward in my spiritual journey. At that time no one else could have done that for me. The ministry flowed out of a unique relationship between Bill and myself. All Christian ministry must flow out of a relationship. Let me explain this.

Jesus is the mediator between God and us. He is our point of contact with God. Now that he has ascended into heaven, Jesus continues to be our mediator but he acts through the fullness of his body. We make up the body of Christ. He is the head; we are the members. We are the mouth of Christ; we are in the hands of Christ. When, in the name of Christ, we lay hands upon another, it is Christ who is touching them through us. When we speak words of comfort to another in his name, it is Christ comforting the other through us. When Bill gave me the space in which to catch my breath it was Christ showing me hospitality.

The biblical notion of hospitality as a sacred duty was based on the Israelites' nomadic life. Deserts are hazardous places to travel in. The desert traveler cannot survive unless those he meets will offer him food, water, and rest in a place of safety. Genesis 18 tells of Abraham, the biblical model of a host. Sitting at the entrance to his tent one hot day Abraham saw three men walking by. He hastened to greet them and urged them to abandon the journey for awhile and rest while he prepared a meal for them. They accepted the invitation. The conversation during the meal reveals that the strangers were in fact God and two angels.

Hospitality is no less necessary for survival today than it was in Abraham's day. The deserts we traverse today are emotional and spiritual rather than physical, but survival is still the issue. We will sometimes need hospitality to survive the rigors of traveling in a spiritual desert. The space I invite the weary spiritual traveler into may be my home, but it is more apt to be my heart. I can offer a friend the hospitality of my heart for a few minutes over a cup of coffee, or while driving to the shopping center together. The ministry of hospitality that I received took place in a home over a period of several weeks. My friend invited me into both his home and his heart.

The ministry of spiritual hospitality is not an easy one. It is a ministry of granting freedom to my guest, freedom to be who she really is. As host I make no demand that my guest live up to my image of what she should be. I do not require her to fill for me the roles she normally fills in daily life. Nor does she need to pretend to be something other than she is at this moment. She does not need to wear a mask for my benefit. I allow her be who she really is.

Bill and his family did not require that I be a "wise and holy priest who had it all together." They did not ask me to offer Mass for them, to hear their confession, to counsel them on spiritual matters. They gave me the precious freedom to be, for the moment, a weary and uncertain spiritual traveler.

Hospitality also means that I don't insist that a guest do the things that I like to do, or to do the things I think would be good for her. And I must let her determine how much togetherness or solitude she wants.

It is hard to give another this much freedom. When you find it hard to allow the person to be who she is, I suggest you concentrate on *enjoying* the person. It is helpful to look at her with new eyes. Concentrate on the strengths and the attributes and gifts that the person has and look for ways to affirm these.

The ministry of hospitality can be especially helpful to children. Most of us can remember some adult other than our parents to whom we could turn in time of difficulty. It may have been a favorite aunt or a grandparent, or perhaps a neighbor. In my neighborhood Mrs. Herley, a widow, had this special gift of hospitality for children. We knew that we could knock at her door anytime and would be welcomed. Most of our visits were casual, but these prepared the way for serious visits in times of confusion and crises. We could ask her questions about religion, or tell her our worries about sex, and troubles at school.

A neighborhood family was going through a divorce. The father had left the home. The mother was beside herself in trying to cope, and was not able to give her children the attention they needed. One of the children, Hilda, was six. Mrs. Herley noticed Hilda's distress and made it known to her that she could come and visit whenever she wanted to. Hilda, now a grown woman, puts it this way:

> "Mrs. Herley saved my life. I was so upset about the breakup of the family. Mom was no help. I was angry at Dad for leaving home, but I felt guilty, too. I thought maybe he wouldn't have left if I'd been better. Mom worried about money so much that I was afraid we might starve. When things got too bad I would go to visit Mrs. Herley. She would show me how to bake cookies, or let me help her clean house. Sometimes she would help me with homework lessons. I would stay overnight sometimes. Only a few times did I tell her what was troubling me, but she seemed to know what I was going through anyway. I don't know what would have happened to me without her."

Hospitality can require of the minister considerable self-sacrifice. Frequently the minister can see the deeper need of her guest and know that she could help, but the guest is not open to deeper ministry. This can be frustrating. The remedy is to respect the person's decision, to know that God's timing is not the same as ours, and to value hospitality as a ministry in its own right and not merely as a means to deeper ministry. The ministry of hospitality may prepare the way for a deeper kind of helping relationship, especially with children who need to feel very comfortable with the minister before they will entrust themselves to him.

If you are a minister of hospitality you must be quite satisfied if nothing beyond hospitality happens. It is a blessing to have given a time of rest and refreshment to a weary traveler. Like Abraham you might find that unknowingly you have entertained God.

13

Giving Comfort

Comforting is an important ministry, but seldom talked about. Comfort, as a ministry, flows out of a relationship characterized by *compassion*. Compassion, a God-given virtue, enables us to feel the distress of another as our own distress. It is, perhaps, the most Christ-like of all virtues. A constant refrain in the Gospels is: "He was moved with compassion," and Jesus takes pains to make certain that we understand that this is the Father's attitude toward all human misfortune. Edward Schillebeeck, a respected theologian, says: "Showing mercy is, despite everything, the deepest purpose that God intends to fulfill in history."

Many situations today call for comfort: a person struggling with economic failure or loss of a job, the death or illness of a loved one, chronic pain or disability, disappointment with a loved one. In these situations the hurting ones need to draw upon the spiritual strength of someone who will stand with them in their suffering.

This is Maria's story of receiving comfort.

"When Tina—she was my youngest—was about two she got very sick. The doctor said she had leukemia and that there was no hope for her. Those were the worst days of my life. Tina would cry or whimper almost all the time and all I could do was sit and rock her. I had to neglect the three older kids and they started acting up to get my attention. My husband couldn't face the fact that Tina was dying and accused me of spoiling her and wanted me to take better care of the house. I almost went crazy.

We had a prayer group at our parish—Healing Waters, they called themselves. One evening some of those ladies came to the house and wanted to pray over Tina. They told us that if we just had faith, Tina would be healed. My husband got pretty sore and told them to *leave us alone*. I guess I wasn't ready for that kind of prayer either. One of them called up later and gave me a bad time for not having enough faith and said if Tina died it would be my fault. I felt so guilty, but my husband was so angry with them that I just couldn't let them come. However, one of them, Laura, called and asked if I could use some help around the house. She said she wouldn't pray or anything like that—just help. I was hesitant but I said 'yes.' She came almost every day for an hour or so. Mostly I would ask her to just hold Tina so I could lie down for an hour. Sometimes I would catch up on housework or do something with the other kids. Once or twice I talked to Laura about how bad I felt. My baby was dying and I could do nothing about it. I guess Laura saved me from losing my mind. She was such a comfort to me."

I asked Maria what she had appreciated most about Laura's help. Maria said:

"She just let us be, and let us work things out in our own way. She didn't give me any advice. But I think the best thing about her was that she was just there—every day. And she could hurt, too. Sometime she would have tears in her eyes when she was holding Tina. I could tell she cared."

The source of Laura's ministry to Maria was compassion. She lessened Maria's pain by her willingness to feel it as her own pain. Comforting is a difficult ministry for twentieth century Americans. We are a doing people and we want immediate solutions. When there are no immediate solutions we feel helpless and not many of us can endure feeling helpless long. The prayer team from Healing Waters felt this helplessness when they were not permitted to help in the only way they could think of— praying for healing. Not able to tolerate feeling helpless, they blamed Maria for these feelings and gave her an additional problem of feeling guilty. Only Laura was able to let go of the "quick fix" solution. This enabled her to think of an alternative way to help. It turned out to be the way of Mary and the Beloved Disciple standing at the foot of the cross: suffering because they were not able to change things for Jesus, but comforting him by their loving presence.

Often the ministry of comforting is one of presence. An arm around the shoulders or holding someone's hand is an important way to be present to another. Listening silently without distraction is another way. Sometimes a quiet reading of Scripture can be powerfully comforting. But it must not be used to avoid sharing the person's pain.

Laura had the courage to offer comfort. To feel Maria's—and Tina's—pain required considerable courage. It is no wonder that we frequently attempt to avoid entering into the person's pain by saying such things as: "Everything will be all right," or "God will not forget you," or "Praise God anyway." Laura had the courage to listen to Maria's pain without cutting her off by trivial reassurances or pious platitudes.

14.

Accepting Self-Disclosure

Matthew, a colleague of mine, tells this story when teaching about accepting self-disclosure.

> "One day my niece, Jean, dropped by and asked me if she could talk to me about an important matter. I invited her in. She began by saying, 'I have this huge logjam blocking me from God. I can't budge it. I can't climb over it, I can't get around it. I need help.'
>
> " 'When did this begin?' I asked.
>
> " 'I did something terrible and I can hardly stand to think about it,' she answered softly. She sat opposite me with her hands clasped tightly in her lap.
>
> " 'Can you tell me what it is? Maybe I can help.'
>
> " 'Well,' she answered, not looking at me, 'you see, I was having a lot of trouble with Mom and I didn't know what to do. I went to a favorite teacher of mine from last year and talked to him about it. He listened to me and then made some suggestions that were so neat I felt like a new person. I wanted him to know how grateful I was, so I thanked him, and then do you know what I did? I threw my arms around his neck and kissed him! And he's a married man! I felt so guilty I could die. I went to confession and the priest said it wasn't a sin, but I still feel guilty. I used to stop by and visit that teacher sometimes, but now I can't go near his room. I blew it.' "

Matthew goes on to say that he encouraged Jean to talk more about her feelings of guilt by acknowledging them as her genuine feelings and that he knew they were painful to her. The discussion that followed enabled her to see her actions in a new light. She was able to see that she had not intended to dishonor the teacher's commitment to his wife, but to express gratitude to him. She also decided that her exprssion of gratitude, while not appropriate, was understandable as girlish enthusiasm. Then Matthew prayed with her that she might accept the Father's love for her.

Matthew ends his story by saying that some weeks later Jean called him and said,

> "Your prayers worked, Uncle. That logjam is gone. Besides that, I have gone back and talked to the teacher and it's O.K. now."

Matthew gave Jean a great gift. His ministry to her can teach us much about accepting another's self-disclosure.

This is a ministry close to the heart of Jesus. He practiced it often. Think of Jesus accepting the outpouring of Mary Magdalene's sorrow when she anointed his feet during a dinner party. We know how this freed her to change her sinful way of life and become the saint God had always intended. Now that he has ascended to the Father, Jesus expects us to continue this ministry. Matthew's listening seriously to Jean's feelings about the "terrible thing" she had done freed her to continue her spiritual journey and to grow into the kind of person God intended.

Secondly, Matthew teaches us how important it is to accept the person's definition of the problem and his or her feelings about it. By telling Jean he heard her pain and accepted her feelings, Matthew enabled her to see her actions through God's eyes. This freed Jean from guilt and enabled her to once again be friends with God and with her teacher. The logjam was broken.

The priest, on the other hand, did not accept Jean's definition of her problem. He dismissed her concern by saying she had not sinned. He was theologically correct, but Jean felt unheard and was left unhelped with her feelings of guilt. I do not mean that we simply leave the person with his or her mistaken opinion. In God's eyes some things are right and some wrong, regardless of our feelings, and we may need to help people accept God's outlook. But this is a goal and we must start where the supplicant is.

Matthew also illustrates an important caution. We can frequently see things about a person that are hidden from that person. It is a mistake to uncover deeper reasons for the problem until the person is ready. For example, Jean's anxiety about kissing her teacher may have been a symptom of unresolved conflicts about her sexuality. But Jean was not ready to look at that and it would have been a mistake for Matthew to have raised that issue.

15.

Instruction

It started at the Thursday night prayer meeting. Rita, with noticeable distress, prayed: "O God, give me the courage to go job-hunting. Please help me: I am so afraid." The group, with some embarrassment, murmured: "Lord, hear this prayer."

Rita was an awkward and immature adolescent who was about to graduate from high school. Her parents were divorced. She lived with her father who suffered from alcoholism. Her mother lived in a distant city. Rita was frightened and confused by the prospect of supporting herself.

When the prayer meeting ended Marion, an experienced legal secretary, walked over to Rita. She offered to coach Rita as she prepared to enter the job market. Rita eagerly accepted the offer. In the following weeks Marion taught her how to dress and use makeup, what to say during a job interview, how to behave in an office, and how to relate to other employees. The prayer group marveled to see this awkward and inept girl blossom into a responsible woman in just a few months.

Marion was ministering "instruction" to Rita. What I mean by instruction is this: to give another the precise information needed at this stage of his or her life's journey. It is different than classroom teaching. Classroom teaching imparts information in a systematic and general way to students for future use. It can be a valuable ministry but is not what I am describing.

Nor am I talking about unsolicited advice giving. Unsolicited advice giving is very common in religious circles, and it is totally useless. Most advice giving is full of "oughts" and "shoulds," which the hearer already knows.

Three principles govern the effectiveness of instruction. First, it must flow out of a special relationship which is important to the person receiving the ministry. Between Marion and Rita there existed this *specialness*. Marion was a mature and successful working woman that Rita could look up to, especially since both shared similar religious values. They had known each other for some time in the prayer group and had common friends and experiences there. Marion saw potential in Rita and liked her. She wanted to help her grow into that potential. Marion had the information and experience that Rita needed at that moment. No one else in Rita's life at that moment could have done for her what Marion did. More often there will be more than one person who can minister instruction effectively, but it cannot be just anyone.

The second principle governing effectiveness is that instruction can only be given at teachable moments in the person's life. The same instruction given a year earlier would not have been helpful to Rita. Marion's coaching was usable to Rita only when she was experiencing anxiety about her future. Before then it would have been unsolicited advice giving. I am not saying that these teachable moments last only a second or an hour or a day. The teachable moment may endure over many months or even many years. But I am saying that there are critical stages in one's life when one is especially open to receive and to make use of instruction in ways that will bring healing or growth.

The third factor governing the effectiveness of instruction is that there is always a struggle to incorporate the new information into one's way of thinking. The struggle was minor with Rita, but for others changing an old habit or thought process can be more difficult.

Philip, a middle-aged Catholic came to see me on the recommendation of a mutual Catholic friend. The friend suggested to Philip that I might be able to help him with his "problem about Holy Communion."

Seated in a chair in my office, Philip was visibly nervous. He said: "I've never talked to a priest like this before."

When I responded that it must be hard to talk about his problem to me, he said: "Yes, but it is a relief too. I've lived with this so long and it's been so hard."

"Will you explain further?" I asked.

"Ten years ago," he began, "my wife divorced me. I didn't want the divorce and I never remarried. I know that when you get a divorce you are automatically excommunicated and are forbidden to receive Holy Communion. I was telling my friend how badly I feel about never being able to receive Holy Communion again and he said I should talk to you."

I informed him that he had misunderstood the teaching of the Catholic Church. Excommunication was attached to remarriage when one was still validly married according to Church law, even though divorced by civil law. It was not attached to the divorce itself.

Philip had some trouble understanding what I was saying so we discussed it in some detail. When he fully understood me, he said: "Are you a liberal or conservative?" He was afraid that I was not presenting the "real" teaching of the Church, but instead a lax personal opinion.

In response, I showed him the law as it was written in a book on Church law. I thought he would be overjoyed at this, but he wasn't. It was so different from what he had believed for so long that he was shaken. Finally he said, "I don't know; can I come back after I think it over?" When he returned the following week he said, "It's hard for me to think about this in a new way, but it would be worse not to receive our Lord out of pride. And I really do want to go to Holy Communion."

I heard his confession and he received Holy Communion at a private Mass I celebrated with his close friend present. Philip was overcome with joy at being able to receive Communion once again. He said to his friend and myself, "You two have given me the best gift I've ever received. Thank you!"

The teachable moment means that there is an urge to move ahead. But at the same time there is the pain of giving up the old way of thinking and acting. The minister of instruction needs to be prepared for the recipient's struggle to accept the new information. Otherwise he might be offended by behavior such as Philip showed toward me on our first meeting. Helping the supplicant to accept the information is part of the ministry.

The ministry of instruction deserves to be more highly valued. It is an important way of helping others. Jesus spent a great deal of time instructing the twelve apostles. The time and care he gave to instructing them bore fruit: it changed their lives, and they in turn changed the course of the world's history.

Jesus continues this ministry of instruction through us as members of his body. I urge ministers of healing prayer to be alert to opportunities to give this kind of help when it is sought. It is not necessary that we have all the information personally, as Marion did. Our job may be to refer the person to someone who is more knowledgeable on this subject, as Philip's friend did for him. We may give someone a book or a pamphlet; we may accompany someone to an agency or to a resource person. But however we impart the information, it must be tailored to the person's situation, and it must flow out a special relationship with the person, and be given at a teachable moment.

SPIRITUAL RESOURCES FOR MINISTERS OF PRAYER

"May (God) enlighten your inmost vision that you may know . . . the immeasurable scope of his power in us who believe. It is like the strength he showed in raising Jesus from the dead" (Eph 1:18–20).

Paul's prayer contains a shocking statement. Am I to believe that I have resurrection power? If so, Paul is right in praying that I may be able to grasp the scope of the power working through me. It is beyond my human ability to believe that I have working in me the same power that raised Jesus from the dead. It is God's power, of course, but it works through us using quite human resources. In this section I want to discuss some of these resources that are channels of God's power working for healing. They are:

1. Prayer of Affirmation
2. Sacramentals
3. Laying On of Hands
4. Resting in the Spirit

16

Prayer of Affirmation

In an earlier chapter the St. Mary's prayer team reported that when they prayed a prayer of affirmation of Larry, he began to sob. For the first time in his life he experienced God approving him. Many of us share with Larry the experience of always thinking we are a disappointment to everyone, especially to God.

Together with Larry we live in a competitive culture that concentrates upon our failures and inadequacies and points them out to us in an effort to make us do better. Parents, teachers, bosses, often criticize our performance, pushing us to do better by belittling what we have done, and by comparing our efforts unfavorably to the accomplishments of siblings, classmates, and fellow workers. They mean well but their constant criticism tears down our self-esteem. Like Larry, we begin to see ourselves as nothing but a failure, and a disappointment to others.

In our culture negative humor is another force that destroys our self-esteem. Our culture teaches us to be very reluctant to give a compliment. And so if we do want to acknowledge an achievement, we frequently use negative humor. This twists the compliment so that it comes out as a put-down. For example a man bowling makes a strike. His partner will probably say: "Well, you finally did something right!" which is really a put-down instead of the compliment it should have been.

Another common practice that is destructive of our self-esteem is discounting. Discounting is diminishing a person's self-esteem to her face. Some examples will make clear what I mean.

A husband discounts his wife when he introduces her to his friends as "just a housewife," or by using unflattering names for her such as "my old lady" or "the war department." He discounts

her when he ignores her suggestions during a discussion as un-
worthy of serious consideration.

Wives discount their husbands, too. I think of a wife in an
informal weekly Bible study whose husband would occasionally
voice an unusual and unique opinion about the meaning of a
Scripture passage. His wife would roll her eyes upward, make a
face and toss her head as if to say: "There goes my dummy
husband again, making a fool of himself."

Parents discount their children. A parent discounts a small
child who has accidentally knocked over a glass of milk by saying
angrily, "You're so clumsy. Can't you do anything right?"

This constant barrage of criticism, negative humor, and discounting so damages our self-esteem that we are not able to
become the person God intends. We feel badly about, and are
highly critical of, ourselves and are not able to see even the goodness in ourselves. We almost always project this self-critical attitude onto others, especially God. Hence we find it difficult to
believe that others, and especially God, approve of us.

And so we begin to believe that all of the criticisms, all of the
negative jokes, all of the discounting statements, are true. We
come to believe what I call the Big Lie. The Big Lie says that we
are of no worth. It becomes a way of life for us. The Big Lie
prevents us from seeing and using the gifts that God has given us
to work for his kingdom. Satan, whom Jesus called the father of
lies, makes use of this deception to further his kingdom.

Thus, the fundamental need of almost every supplicant will
be the healing of her wounded self-esteem. And affirmation is an
especially powerful resource given to us by God to achieve this
healing.

There are three steps in affirmation. The first is to see the
goodness that is in a person as a gift from God. The second is to
allow yourself to be so moved by seeing that goodness that you
give thanks to God for the person. The third step is to express that
thanksgiving in some external way to the person himself. In ministry you can do this by a direct statement, or by the prayer of
affirmation.

Direct positive feedback about the goodness we see in a person is affirming. Most people receive so little positive feedback

and are so critical of themselves that they need help to recognize the gifts they have. You might say directly to a supplicant, "You have such a lovely gift of deep trust in God's desire to heal you. Your trust builds up my faith. Thank you."

Another way to externalize one's thankfulness for the supplicant's goodness is by a prayer of affirmation. Here the minister gives thanks directly to God for the supplicant, in the supplicant's presence. I remember the prayer of affirmation that I was moved to say for Genevieve.

Life was hard for Genevieve. She was the single parent, working mother, of five children. I had known her for several years when she asked me to pray with her. Her fourteen year old daughter was being "mouthy." Genevieve had become furious and had slapped her. Her reaction frightened her. She herself had been a physically abused child and she feared that she might repeat the pattern of physical abuse. I prayed something like this.

> "Father in heaven, I give you thanks for Genevieve. I thank you for the gift she is to her family. I thank you for the joy with which she takes care of her family. I thank you for the ready smile she has in times of difficulty. I thank you that you have gifted her with a heart that is open to others in their times of trial and pain. Father, I thank you for the deep faith that Genevieve has in the healing power of your Son Jesus. I thank you for the courage she has to step forward in faith and ask for healing."

A caution is in order. Affirmation must not degenerate into empty flattery or trite phrases. The supplicant would sense its phoniness and this would damage the supplicant's trust in the minister. Affirmation is not a technique that we can use at will. It is a prayer by which we praise God for his handiwork. The prayer of affirmation, like the prayer of praise, is the work of the Holy Spirit. We cannot pray on our own power. St. Paul tells us that we cannot so much as proclaim that "Jesus is Lord" except by the power of the Holy Spirit (2 Cor. 12:3). If I find myself praying the same thing about each person, or if I can't think of anything to affirm, these are signs that I need to pray that the Holy Spirit revive in me the gift of affirmation. For this to happen I may need to spend time in private prayer praising God for each supplicant. I must pray frequently that God's gift of affirmation will grow so strong in me that affirmation will become my way of life.

17.

Sacramentals

Sacramentals are another valuable resource for the minister of healing prayer. Those most frequently used are holy water, blessed oil, salt, candles, the cross, banners, and flowers. Through our use of them God makes real to us his presence, beauty, and power. A correct understanding of sacramentals will help the minister use them effectively.

The prototype for all sacramentals is the incarnation—the Word made flesh. When God decided to become present to his people in a new and unique way—through the Son taking on human nature—something totally new happened. The invisible and intangible reality of God is now made known to us through the visible human life of Jesus of Nazareth. Jesus himself put it in its simplest terms when he said: "Whoever has seen me has seen the Father" (Jn 14:9).

But Jesus, knowing that he was going to ascend to the Father after his death and resurrection, was concerned about future generations who would not see him in the flesh. So he gave us the sacraments. Their use by the Christian community would continue his presence among us and would impart a share of his divine life to us. The sacraments are ordinarily administered only by an ordained minister when the Christian community is gathered in an official way: for example, the Eucharist celebrated in church on Sunday.

Since Christians often have the need of symbols in their everyday life to remind them of the continued presence and power of Christ, over the centuries the Christian community has followed the example of Jesus and made use of other symbols in addition to the ones Jesus gave us. These we call sacramentals. They are articles of everyday use—water, oil, salt, candles—made holy by the prayer of the Christian community: that is to say, they are blessed. When these blessed articles are used "in faith" they are one of the ways that Christ's presence and power in our everyday life is made more real.

Magical thinking about sacramentals is a real danger, but clarity about their true meaning will help us use this powerful resource correctly. They are to be used "in faith." Our faith in using them is in God's benevolence and power. We do not believe that they have a power in themselves with which we can control our environment. That would be the practice of magic. Rather they are intended to stimulate our faith in Christ's power. For example, when I light a blessed candle as a holy symbol, I am reminded that Christ is present as the light of the world, and that it is he who overcomes the darkness. We bring faith to the use of sacramentals, but their very use stirs us to even greater faith.

For example, when I bless myself, or others, with holy water I am reminded that I have been baptized into Christ and am a well-loved child of God.

Ministers of healing sometimes ask how they can know which sacramental to use. The question betrays a wrong understanding of sacramentals. They are not like a doctor's prescription of medicine for a certain ailment. Each medicine has a particular effect: it changes the chemistry of the body in a special way. Sacramentals work differently. They work by way of symbolism. Their use is guided by the way a particular symbol will affect a supplicant. The proper question to ask is, "Will this sacramental help this supplicant experience Christ as present to him in love, and with power to meet his need?"

Admittedly this is not an simple guideline. It may be difficult to know what meaning a certain sacramental will have for this supplicant. Another difficulty is that each sacramental symbolizes many different things. Water, for example, because it is the source of all life, is a symbol for God's gift of divine life. But because it is also a natural cleansing agent, it symbolizes the forgiveness of sin. Again, on the natural level water symbolizes refreshment: when we are weary we take a leisurely shower or hot bath. And so it can carry the meaning of the Holy Spirit refreshing us in times of spiritual weariness.

Some examples of how I have used each of the common sacramentals may be helpful to you.

Blessed Water

Blessed water's many symbolic meanings make this sacramental a powerful aid in the ministry of healing. For example, bathing the head of a person who is physically sick and weak is a sign that Jesus is giving them more of his abundant life. Blessed water carries the meaning of refreshment for a supplicant who is weary from a long struggle with drug addiction. Reading to the supplicant the words of Jesus, "Come to me, all of you who are tired from carrying heavy loads, and I will refresh you" (Mt 11:28), as you bless him with the holy water would strengthen its meaning.

I like to bless myself and the team as we prepare for ministry to remind ourselves that we have been baptized in Christ and are gathering as his people to minister in his name. When ministry is especially difficult, making the sign of the cross upon oneself or the supplicant with holy water helps. This gesture reminds us that Jesus has won the victory over all evil by his cross and resurrection. Sometimes during ministry we experience an especially intense activity of evil spirits attempting to hinder the ministry. When this occurs we sprinkle our surroundings and ourselves to remind us that Jesus has defeated Satan.

The symbolism of water as a cleansing agent was of great help in ministering to a woman who had been sexually assaulted. She could not get free of feeling violated. As she expressed it, "I feel dirty and damaged." Sex, for her, had become so confused with violence that even sex with her loving husband was a torment for her. I suggested that she draw a tub of warm water, pour in a bottle of holy water which I gave her, and soak in it as she prayed. I instructed her how to use imagery in prayer. We discussed the kind of images that she felt comfortable in using. She chose to image herself as an infant being bathed tenderly by Mary with Jesus, as her older brother, present. She visualized the power of Jesus to cleanse and to heal being present in the bath water. She did this every day for a week. She reported that it contributed to remarkable progress in being healed of those destructive feelings about herself and sex.

Blessed Oil

The official book of blessing prayers for the Roman Catholic Church contains a blessing for oil to be used by the laity. It is this oil that I am speaking of here. I am not speaking of the oil blessed by a bishop (in some special circumstances by a priest) to be used in administering the sacrament of anointing of the sick. In Roman Catholic thought a clear distinction between the two blessings is important because the administration of the sacrament of anointing of the sick is reserved to an ordained priest, and the oil blessed for that sacrament must not be used by a non-ordained minister. The Catholic lay minister must take care in using oil blessed for lay use that the recipient of her ministry not think that he has received the sacrament of the anointing of the sick. Roman Catholic bishops and priests are rightly concerned about any confusion regarding the official sacraments.

But with that caution in mind, the use of blessed oil plays an important role in the ministry of healing prayer. Oil has two symbolic meanings that are important in ministry: healing and consecration.

In biblical times oil was used to heal wounds. Even today oil is used in healing ointments as the basic ingredient in lotions for the massage of aching muscles and to prevent bedsores in hospital patients. The symbolism of oil, as a soothing and healing agent, makes it useful in the ministry of prayer for physical healing. The minister can rub it on, or near, the afflicted part of the body if that can be decently done. Or the supplicant himself can do so. Otherwise it may be applied to the forehead as standing for the whole person. The application is accompanied with a prayer for healing that will stir up faith that God will use this sacramental as a means of healing. A good practice is to give the supplicant a small bottle of oil to use as she continues to pray for healing at home.

But the blessed oil may also be used in ministering to emotional, spiritual or relational wounds. In ministering to someone who is brokenhearted, I ask her to anoint herself over her heart while I pray that the Lord heal her brokenness. In praying for healing of memories I annoint the supplicant's forehead.

In biblical times oil was used to consecrate a person to be king, priest, and prophet. Even today it is used in the coronation ceremony of the king or queen of England, and is used in liturgical churches to ordain its ministers. This meaning of blessed oil as an agent of consecration makes it useful in commissioning the supplicant for some special task as part of spiritual or relational healing. I might, for example, anoint the supplicant as I pray that the Lord will strenthen him to fulfill his family role when the wound is a relational one between husband and wife, or parent and child.

Blessed Candles

I have a special affection for blessed candles. They were a part of everyday religious life in my family. When a thunderstorm was coming my mother would tell me to light the blessed candle and to say a prayer for protection. Lighting the candle was a great privilege for me. And as the darkness of the storm with frightening flashes of lightning and peals of thunder broke upon us, the burning candle made it easier for me to believe that Christ was present and would protect us.

A lighted candle has more than one symbolic meaning. It reminds us that Jesus is the light of the world and that he has overcome the darkness. It is also a symbol of welcoming. For a special person or for a special occasion we set the dinner table with lighted candles. During the ministry we have lighted candles in the room to welcome the supplicant as a special person and to remind her that Christ is present.

As the team begins to prepare itself for ministry, lighting a candle signals a change. Social conversation is ended. The team is drawn into a conscious recognition of God's presence. A lighted candle transforms an ordinary room into a sacred place. Faith is aroused. We can more easily believe that Jesus is with us in this ministry.

A lighted candle—or, even better, several of them—is a way

of welcoming the supplicant into the place of ministry. It signals that she is a special person and that this is a special occasion. It helps draw her into the presence of God.

The team will sometimes place a candle in the hands of a supplicant during ministry when things seem especially painful or hopeless for her, or when she is being commissioned to be a light to others as a result of her healing.

Candles, in fact all sacramentals, are especially helpful when ministering to young children. Symbols will convey God's presence and care when words won't. You may need to invent sacramentals for them. One team blessed helium filled balloons. They then tied symbols of the child's hurts on them and had the child go outdoors and release them to indicate that Jesus would take the hurts away.

Blessed Salt

Salt as a natural element carries symbolic meanings that are important in the ministry of healing prayer. It is a condiment used to enhance the flavor of food. Jesus had this use of salt in mind when he called his disciples "the salt of the earth." Salt is used as a preservative to keep food from spoiling. It is sometimes used as an antiseptic to prevent infection of a wound. Mindful of these meanings, Christians use blessed salt to combat Satan and other forces of evil. So when the supplicant is involved in a spiritual or moral struggle, blessed salt is a valuable sacramental. The team might sprinkle the place of ministry with blessed salt during the preparation time. The team itself or the supplicant could be sprinkled during ministry. I have used it successfully with supplicants who are struggling to break addiction to nicotine. I give the supplicant a small vial of blessed salt and recommend that he place a few grains on his tongue and call upon the Lord to meet his needs when he craves nicotine.

18.

Laying on Hands

Jesus laid hands upon the sick and healed them. He commanded his disciples to do likewise. Behind the ritual of laying on hands is the fundamental importance of touch for human beings. A human being simply cannot survive if totally isolated from other creatures. And touch is the most elementary way of being connected to others. Each square inch of skin has millions of receptors that are constantly taking in messages from the environment. We know, for example, that touch is essential to the process of bonding the mother and her newborn infant. Without this connectedness to another human person the infant will not do well and will sometimes even die for no medical reason. Dolores Krieger has established the value of touch by hospital nurses. Her research indicates that when nurses use therapeutic touch on hospital patients the chemical composition of their blood actually changes.

The experience of being touched has not only physiological and psychological effects, but spiritual ones as well. Jesus was certainly aware of this. He used touch in ways other than the ritual of laying on hands. Think of his hugging the little children who were brought to him for a blessing. Mark tells us that Jesus reached out and actually touched the leper—perhaps embraced him: a powerful way of reconnecting the man who has been ostracized from all human connectedness for the entire time of his illness.

So it is not surprising that many of the principal religious activities in Christianity involve touching. In Roman Catholic practice, every one of the seven sacraments involve some form of ritual touching.

In the ministry of healing prayer touch may be administered

in a ceremonial way with the hands extended and laid lightly upon the head or shoulders of the supplicant. But a more common way is to hold the person's hand, or place your arm around his shoulders, while seated close to him. On occasion it may be appropriate to embrace the supplicant, or even to hold him. This would be done, for example, when the supplicant is sobbing in grief or other pain. In praying for a child you might take him upon your lap.

There are some cautions, however, in using touch. Before using it make sure that the supplicant is comfortable with touch. For a variety of reasons some people are not comfortable with it, or even with physical closeness. To some supplicants, sitting too close to them seems like a violation of their "space." Sometimes you can tell by people's body language that they are uncomfortable with closeness or touch. They may move away from you, or tense up when you come close. Perhaps the safest way is simply to ask the supplicants if they are uncomfortable with touch or closeness. Do not assume you know the answer to this question even if the person is a member of a group that customarily hugs. Some people simply endure hugging but are uncomfortable with it. If this is so, touch will hinder ministry.

Another caution is in order. Touch can have sexual meanings. Any use of touch in ministry that can carry a sexual meaning, such as hugging a person too closely for too long, touching the upper thigh, or kissing on the lips, is entirely inappropriate. Ministry by a team is a safeguard against these meanings, but may not entirely eliminate them.

Even an innocent use of touch can evoke negative feelings. On one occasion in ministering as a member of a team, I unthinkingly laid my hand upon the supplicant's shoulder as she was sobbing. She flinched and drew back. I withdrew my hand and later asked her if she was uncomfortable with touch. She said that as a child she had been sexually abused by her father. In such a situation touch of any kind is inadvisable.

But most people respond favorably to the use of touch in ministry. It is such a powerful way of becoming connected and most supplicants want to feel closely connected to the ministers.

Touch is a way of communicating. We can pick up information from supplicants by touch. We can tell if they are tense or relaxed. We can tell when changes take place as we minister to them. But we also give information about ourselves to the supplicant by laying on hands. So the laying on of hands must be an expression of love. The hands must be laid on gently and with respect. I have experienced ministers of healing laying their hands upon me so heavily that it was a burden. I did not feel respected but felt that I was an object being dominated by the ministers. Needless to say, it was not a healing experience.

19

Resting in the Spirit

Resting in the Spirit is a valuable means of healing for prayer teams. It is sometimes referred to as being *Slain in the Spirit* or *Overcome by the Spirit*. It can occur at special moments when the person is so filled with the power of the Spirit that the body and the mind needs to "rest" from other activities. It happens most often when the person is being prayed for and falls over backward. A superficial observer might think that the "resting" person has fainted and is unconscious. But this is not so. The person is more acutely conscious than usual. But his consciousness is focused on God's activity within, and he is filtering out external distractions such as conversations and activities around him. He could pay attention to them if he cared to, but is generally uninterested in doing so. He is so preoccupied with what God is doing within that he has no energy for other considerations. Psychology would call this an altered state of consciousness.

Ministers of healing sometimes so "superspiritualize" Resting in the Spirit that they leave no room for a natural dimension in it. The best understanding of it is that it is a natural spiritual phenomenon used by God at special times for his own special purposes. The causes of it are complex and not fully known, but we do know some things about them. Almost certainly the causes are a mixture of divine and human. Sometimes the human element can be a greater part of the cause than at other times. For example human expectancy can be part of the cause, and if people come to a large healing service with the expectation that it will happen, and are even eager to experience it, it is more likely to happen. Another example of the human element is "group contagion." If it happens to several people in a group, it is likely to spread to others.

Some ministers of healing use Resting in the Spirit primarily as a demonstration of God's power. Since it demonstrates the power of God in a highly dramatic way, they think it should be used to increase expectancy that God will heal in miraculous ways. I think this is a dangerous abuse based on a wrong understanding of it. It only fosters a wrong understanding of the ministry of healing prayer.

I view Resting in the Spirit as a valuable aid to healing to be used only privately. The supplicant Resting in the Spirit is less distracted and less self-conscious, and this allows the Spirit to operate in her more fully. I believe that Resting in the Spirit should *not* be used in large public gatherings. The person Resting in the Spirit may need personal attention which cannot be given in mass meetings. If this needed personal ministry is not available, Resting in the Spirit, can be a destructive, rather than a healing, experience.

Because the causes of Resting in the Spirit are a mixture of the divine and human, the ministers and the supplicant have some, though not total, control of the situation. The ministers can create an atmosphere which will facilitate the work of the Spirit in the supplicant. And usually the supplicant can choose to accept or to resist the experience to some degree.

Some people report that the experience is so powerful that they are unable to resist it, or even to "come out of it" by their own volition. However, I think it more likely that the experience of God is so gratifying that they are unwilling, at some deep level, to resist or to "come out of it." If an overriding emergency required, I believe they could do so.

People report a wide range of experiences associated with Resting in the Spirit. If the supplicant is Resting in the Spirit from a standing position, he will feel as though he is floating to the ground. This is deceptive because in fact he is not floating, but falling. The fall could injure him, and so it is necessary to have someone standing behind him strong enough to catch him and lower him safely to the floor. The person may rest there from several seconds to several hours. While "resting" some enjoy a sense of quiet and peace. And although nothing special seems to be happening, they are content to remain in that state for some

time. Some experience happiness, joy, or even mirth. One supplicant reported experiencing the Holy Spirit as water flowing over
her entire being, refreshing and cleansing her. An experience of
the Divine Presence in the form of brilliant light or colors is
common. Others report Jesus present, effecting physical, emotional or spiritual healing. It is not unusual for people to cry tears
of relief or joy.

Occasionally someone will have a bad experience. She will
get in touch with painful memories that have not been healed
and will need someone to minister to her while she continues
Resting in the Spirit. Although it is not frequent a person may
discover that she is troubled by the influence of evil spirits and
will need the ministry of deliverance.

We include Resting in the Spirit in our training program. We
provide each student with the opportunity to Rest in the Spirit
himself, and to minister it to another. This is done in the training
group under the supervision of the staff. This training takes it out
of the realm of the sensational and gives the students a solid basis
for using it as a resource in their ministry.

The following letter reports what happened to one student
when she Rested in the Spirit during this "practice" session.

Dear Fr. Leo,
    I'd like to share with you my own experience in Resting in
the Spirit during our training session.
    I remember your praying for me to receive any gift that
God had to give. The next thing I was aware of was a beautiful,
elderly man looking me directly in the face and saying, "Mary,
you can trust me." He then took my hand and helped me to my
feet. (I was still physically lying down.) Before I go any further
I want to tell you about this man. I knew when I first saw him
that he was ageless; no beginning and no ending. His hair was
white and seemed to glow. His eyes were as fire—fire that has
burned a very long time. His skin was smooth. Still he was
very old and luminous. His whole being and countenance was
love: love so deep that it came from deep burning.
    After he had helped me to my feet, we were standing side
by side. He then began to show me my life: from the moment
of conception to now. As my life began to unfold I was stand-

ing aside and Jesus was experiencing the things that have happened to me.

I saw myself being beaten and I was going untouched. I saw him being molested and raped and I was unwounded. I saw him experiencing the inability to speak, to walk, to communicate, and I was not scared. I saw him frozen in fear and in terror and I was able to live, to desire life. I saw him become the adult I became, bitter, frightened, full of grief, I saw that I was no longer that way—that I had become a different person than the events of my life had caused me to be.

Later as I grasped the horror that was happening I wanted to rescue Jesus. But I just stood there while this beautiful old man held my hand. Throughout this part it seemed that his strength was pouring into me as he held my hand.

While all this was going on there was a tremendous noise, like a boom when the sound barrier is broken. It seemed that every molecule of my being was being changed.

Father, this has stayed with me. Three weeks have passed since I first began to set this down. Finally it is all down.

God bless you,

(Signed)

How To Minister Resting in the Spirit

If this is the first time the team has used it with this supplicant, one of the team explains to the supplicant what Resting in the Spirit is, what it feels like, and why the team thinks it would be beneficial. The supplicant is asked if he is willing to Rest in the Spirit. The team should not proceed with it if the supplicant indicates any unwillingness. The instruction should place emphasis on a desire for the Lord's healing presence, and not create a fascination with the experience itself.

In ministering Resting in the Spirit, the supplicant would ordinarily start in a standing position while those ministering to him would stand before him, with one or two strong people behind to catch him when he falls. The ministers should not actually lay their hands upon the head of the supplicant so there is no feeling of being pushed over. Rather the hands are held close to the forehead while the team prays, audibly but quietly, that the person will experience an infilling of the Holy Spirit. Music and song may be used. Prayer in one's prayer language is useful if the supplicant is comfortable with it. Prayer in the vernacular requesting God to heal the supplicant is useful. This kind of prayer might last anywhere from two to five minutes. If "Resting" does not happen within that time, the team does not persist in prayer. To do so only causes tension for everyone. Sometimes a brief conversation with the supplicant will disclose some obstacle that can be dispelled through conversation. The team can then pray once again for the supplicant, and many times he does then experience Resting in the Spirit. But if not, the team will have informed the supplicant ahead of time that he may or may not experience Resting in the Spirit and that if it does not happen this is not to be considered a failure.

When the supplicant falls back she is caught and gently lowered to the floor and covered with a blanket. The purpose of covering the supplicant is to make her feel more secure. Lying on the floor before others causes one to feel vulnerable. And some supplicants worry about undignified appearance. Being covered reduces these preoccupations.

We have discovered that it is quite possible to Rest in the Spirit starting from a position of sitting on the floor with one's legs extended so that only the upper part of the body falls backward. This is useful when the supplicant is especially heavy, or the members too few or too weak to catch the supplicant, or the supplicant is fearful of injuring himself in a fall. We have also discovered that it is possible to start from a prone position, but this seems to work well only when the person has previously experienced some actual falling. Allowing oneself to fall seems to be a symbolic action of letting go of control of one's life and giving it over to God. After one has once had the experience of surrendering, it then seems possible to Rest in the Spirit while lying down. If you are praying for a person to "Rest" from the prone position it is necessary to have your hands upon him to detect the perceptible release of muscle tension which is a signal that "Resting" has occurred.

Instruct the supplicant that once she is Resting in the Spirit, she should occasionally and briefly tell the team what she is experiencing so that they can decide what direction their continued ministry should take. If God's presence is intense and healing, the team should merely pray quietly for the healing to continue. The supplicant's occasional brief reports will guide the team's prayer.

If after Resting in the Spirit nothing much seems to be happening, the team should quietly proceed according to the plan of action previously decided upon, with the supplicant still "Resting." Any one of the four areas, physical, emotional, spiritual, or relational, can be ministered to. It is not wise to enter into any long discussion with the supplicant while he is Resting in the Spirit. The team may ask him to report what he is experiencing in the way of images, experiences of God, and memories so that their ministry will not hinder what the Spirit is doing. Occasionally the team will suggest images or report to the supplicant images or thoughts they believe are from the Lord.

Sometimes Resting in the Spirit will bring healing when nothing else works. Our team was stymied with Ruth. Nothing was working. She had grown up in a violent family and had been physically and emotionally abused. Although badly depressed and suicidal, she had a close relationship with God and desperately wanted to be healed. (She was under psychiatric care, and her psychiatrist knew of our ministry.) Yet whenever a team member would ask even a simple clarifying question Ruth would become argumentative and the team would get involved in the argument and all of us would become confused. Although we discussed this with the supplicant she seemed unable to control this behavior. So we decided to avoid all discussion and use only Resting in the Spirit. Ruth agreed to this.

Since she had not experienced it before we told her what the procedure would be, what Resting in the Spirit was like, and how she could cooperate with the Spirit's healing presence.

We started with a generous time of praise, using music and song as well as praise prayers. With Ruth standing we then prayed directly that she might be so filled with the Spirit that she would "Rest" in his presence. This she did quickly. We covered her with a blanket and sat on the floor near her. I occasionally asked her to report what was happening. She would briefly describe her experience: usually in terms of flowing water and brilliantly colored light. She reported being intensely aware of God's presence. Only rarely did we make a suggestions to direct her use of imagery. Mostly we prayed quietly, even silently, sometimes using our prayer language. Occasionally we used recorded instrumental music as we prayed.

We would minister in this way for about forty-five minutes. We would tell her when the time was drawing to an end to give her time to come out of the "Resting" state. Once she was roused we gave her time to give additional reports of what had happened if she wished, but we did not ask questions and did not discuss what she had reported. We would spend a short time giving thanks to God for what he had done with Ruth. We would arrange a time for our next meeting and Ruth would leave.

We ended our ministry with Ruth after the eighth of these sessions. Both Ruth and the team felt that she was sufficiently healed to live out her Christian life productively, and this proved to be the case.

One of the team members had occasional informal contact with Ruth and reported that she continued to show signs of progressive healing over the next several years. Ruth found new joy in life and a new energy that allowed her to undertake a difficult ministry: she opened a shelter for homeless women.

I have discussed four resources—Prayer of Affirmation, Sacramentals, Laying On of Hands, and Resting in the Spirit— that are especially helpful in the ministry of healing prayer. They have been given to us by God, and through their use in faith he heals the hurts of his wounded children. I join my prayer with St. Paul's that all of us may come to know the immeasurable scope of his power resident in our ministry to the wounded and sorrowful members of Christ's body.

THE MINISTER OF HEALING

20.

Qualities and Training of a Minister of Healing Prayer

The voice coming from the telephone receiver was that of a woman, probably in her late forties, and she identified herself as Lila. I didn't know her. She said, "Father, God has given me a healing ministry and I want to work with you."

This was not the first time I had received such a call, but even so I did not know what to say. I knew what she expected of me: she expected that I would rejoice with a "Praise the Lord, Sister Lila.": But I was deeply suspicious and did not want to be falsely encouraging. I weakly replied that I directed a two year program of training for the healing ministry and would be glad to send her a flyer describing the program.

I got the expected response from her. "Father, you don't understand. When I was baptized in the Holy Spirit I received the gift of healing. *God* has given me this ministry. I don't need training."

I responded, "That may be so but the Christian community needs to discern the authenticity of that gift and you need to develop the gift, and that takes time and training." She responded with the predictable arguments that I had heard before. I countered them. She finally accused me of being unspiritual and a secular humanist and hung up in anger.

I was sad. I knew from previous experience what would likely happen. She would launch out on a "lone ranger" ministry, grind up a number of vulnerable hurting souls who accepted her ministry, alienate several clergy, and further discredit the ministry of healing prayer. In the end she would become embittered and withdraw from the institutional Church in anger.

Now I *do* believe that God calls people to the ministry of healing prayer and I *do* believe that he bestows gifts of healing upon the body of Christ. But I also know that even someone so dramatically called as St. Paul spent three years in Arabia, presumably readying himself for ministry by prayer and study. He started his ministry not as a "lone ranger" but when he was called to it by the Christian community at Antioch through the person of Barnabas. I know, too, that all the major Christian denominations require a long period of training, and demonstrated competence, before they ordain their ministers.

Lila might have developed into a minister of healing prayer if she had been docile enough to have taken the time to discern and to develop her gifts. But her lack of docility would deprive the body of Christ of a meaningful ministry.

But another type of person also deprives the body of Christ of healing ministry. Their inadequate response to God's call is seldom noticed. These are the souls so timid that it never even occurs to them that God might call them to any kind of ministry. If someone brings this to their attention they excuse themselves by saying that they are not worthy to be used by God. Corrine was such a person.

Corrine was a member of a parish I served on Sundays. She was unassuming but friendly and with a pleasant personality. She had been asked by the pastor years ago to take care of the altar linen, and to prepare the altar for Mass each day. She had done this faithfully ever since. She usually spent time praying before the Blessed Sacrament both before and after Mass. I noticed how her attentiveness to visitors and newcomers during the social hour would cause them to brighten up. She impressed me as a mature Christian with potential as a minister of healing. So I gave her a flyer describing our program of training and asked her to consider taking part in it.

She expressed surprise and some anxiety, saying, "I could never pray out loud for people." I said, "Maybe not, but I think you would profit from the course personally and maybe you would discover some new gifts." I suggested that she talk with Marie, a fellow parishioner whom she knew and who had been in the training program. I didn't push the matter any further, but she did talk to Marie and did enroll in the first year of the program.

I saw Corrine nearly every Sunday but she never talked about the program until the end of the year. Then she thanked me for encouraging her to enroll in the program. She said that the first year had been a time of spiritual growth for her. Reading the assigned books and doing the individual self-reflection exercises had opened her eyes to new avenues of spiritual growth. I knew from the report of other trainees that her reflection group valued her quiet wisdom and genial personality, and that she had grown in self-confidence.

Although she hesitated about enrolling in the second year of the program—because she would now have to pray as a member of a healing team for supplicants—she finally did so. She proved to be an effective and valued member of her team. Supplicants responded positively to her deep compassion for their pain and her ability to be a nurturing person. Her deep love for Jesus was apparent in her simply stated prayers.

At the beginning of the training program the following fall she volunteered to help with registrations at the opening retreat. I gladly accepted this offer, but also asked her if she would act as leader of one of the prayer teams in training. She asked for time to pray about it. The next Sunday she said, "I am scared of being a leader, but I have received so much benefit that I should help others to receive it. So, yes, I will lead a group."

Except for her lack of self-confidence, Corrine had all the qualities needed to be an excellent team leader. The training staff member who supervised Corrine's prayer team gave her a lot of feedback pointing out her positive qualities as a team leader. This helped her grow in self-confidence. Over the year she became an excellent leader. Her two outstanding leadership gifts were common sense wisdom and the ability to draw out the other team members' gifts.

At the end of the year I asked her if she had considered forming a team to minister in her parish. She said that she had but didn't know how to go about it. She asked, "Would you help me form the team and would you talk to my pastor?"

Eight other trainees had made a similar request, so I set up a half-day conference on starting healing teams in one's own parish. Out of this conference Corrine found a man and a woman who joined her as a team. She contacted the pastor to discuss the ministry they would offer, and I supported their efforts by a letter to the pastor describing the training they had had, their qualifications and the kind of ministry I thought them to be capable of. Out of this they received his cautious approval for a trial period of six months after which he would review their ministry with them.

Although there have been some changes in the composition of Corrine's team it has been functioning now for several years and they have the wholehearted approval of the pastor who found their ministry to be a valuable resource for the parish.

Corrine is representative of many people's lack of awareness of their gifts. Only slowly, with the help of others, did she recognize them and become willing to put them at the service of the body of Christ.

But there is a different experience, often associated with the charismatic renewal movement. An important part of this movement's spirituality is to provide for a powerful experience of the release of the power of the Holy Spirit in people's lives. This experience is called by a variety of names; baptism in the Holy Spirit, release of the Holy Spirit and pentecostal experience. Lila had such an experience, and gifts of healing may have been released in her by the experience. But spiritual power, like all other forms of power, can be used well or badly. The gifts associated with the ministry of healing are especially prone to these destructive uses. A great temptation is to use them to bolster one's own ego by gaining the recognition of others as a special person, or by exercising control over their lives in God's name.

What Lila needed was a long period of using the traditional Christian disciplines of prayer, study, and accountability to enable her to use her newly released spiritual gifts constructively. But Lila was not willing to undergo the discipline of learning how to use God's gift for the good of others and to discipline her own needs so they didn't get in the way.

Lila made another mistake. She put all the emphasis on the charism of healing and refused to value and to develop both her natural gifts and her God-given virtues such as faith, love, prudence, and fortitude. This is a mistake because the effective use of the charisms must build upon one's natural gifts and virtues. Lila was squandering the gifts God was offering to the Christian community through her.

Corrine, too, was in danger of squandering God's gift of healing by not paying attention to, and developing, the God-given virtue of fortitude. Her timidity prevented her from seeing the gifts that God had given her. However, eventually she was able to heed God's call because she had learned the Christian disciplines of regular prayer and quiet service to others.

Qualities of a Healing Person

Although God makes uses of all kinds of unlikely people to do his work, there does seem to be a core of qualities needed to be a minister of healing prayer. I think that the nucleus of this core is the ability to lead the supplicant into an experience of Jesus meeting her in her need. From this nucleus then flows several other core qualities and these will differ according to the culture and personality of the supplicant. No one person can lead everyone into an experience of Jesus. But the irreducible core of qualities that are needed to do so are:

(1) a lively, vivid, and personal relationship with Jesus that has been matured through the practice of the traditional Christian disciplines;
(2) the ability to listen deeply to the supplicant as he tells his story;
(3) the motivation of compassion for exercising this ministry;
(4) the knowledge and skill to put this compassion to work to heal the wounds that the supplicant has brought to her.

Training for Team Ministry

A description of the program, "Formation for Healing Ministry," offered by the Institute for Christian Ministries, will give you an idea of the training we believe is necessary to prepare for a public ministry of healing prayer.

It is offered on weekends and evenings so that the trainee does not need to interrupt other obligations of work and family. It spans a period of two years. The first year is oriented principally to instruction but incorporates experience and spiritual formation into it. The student is expected to read at least six books, listen to twenty-four presentations, attend two weekend retreats, and participate in eighteen group meetings in which one student's ministry is reviewed each meeting. All this totals to something like eighty classroom hours for the first year.

The second year is oriented to actual practice of team ministry, although reading, listening to lectures, and personal spiritual growth are still part of the program. Each trainee is assigned to a team guided by a trained leader. Each team offers ministry twenty-four times for about an hour each time under the personal supervision of a staff member. In this second year, through feedback from other team members and the supervisor, and by personal prayerful reflection, the trainee is encouraged to discern whether or not God is calling her to this ministry. As we saw in Corrine's case this is not always clear even at the end of the second year. The more usual way for the call to be heard is by experimentation and circumstances and subsequent reflection on one's ministry.

What the above description does not make clear is the spiritual formation that takes place during these two years. Except for the times of worship that are part of every meeting and of the retreats, there is no one element of the program that is termed "spiritual formation." Rather it is built into every element of the program. However, students report that one element—the written self-reflection exercises that follow upon the assigned readings—have a great impact upon their spiritual lives. They also report that the group meetings that reflect upon one's ministry have a strong formative effect on their spiritual lives.

But without a doubt the biggest impact happens in the times of actual ministry. The experience of seeing God at work in the lives of supplicants through one's own ministry is a powerful force in one's spiritual life.

The trainees tell us repeatedly in their evaluations at the end of the program that their own lives have been radically changed as a result of two years of training and the practice of ministry. One of our students wrote in her final evaluation:

> "During the past year I participated in the Formation for Healing Ministry program. This program through readings, lectures, group participation and written exercises has deepened, integrated, and centered my life more deeply in Jesus. I feel that I have received new life. I don't look back on the past with sorrow and pain but instead with joy and thanksgiving to God for his great love for me. I embrace the past. Through it he has gifted me and graced me. I feel whole.
>
> Today I have a strong belief that nothing happens or is so terrible that good cannot come out of it. God doesn't cause the tragedy or trauma but he is in it loving me, strengthening me, gifting me if I allow him and am willing to let go of revengefulness, resentment, and am able to forgive.
>
> It is through and out of participation in this program that I sense my calling and desire to give of what I have received—to reach out to the sick, lonely, and hurting people."

Appendix A:

Checklist for Self-Evaluation of Prayer Team Ministry

I. **Physical Setting**
   1. Decorations and arrangement to create the sense of a holy place.
   2. Creation of a spiritually warm, inviting space by the team.

II. **Preparation Phase**
   1. Leader checks the readiness of the team members to minister.
   2. Team members set aside any concerns by giving them to the Lord in prayer.
   3. Leader helps the team form a bond of unity and mutual love.
   4. Team focuses on preparation for ministry, leaving other kinds of sharing for other times.
   5. A brief review of the previous prayer time and plan for this session.
   6. Enough prayer time to get the team "in tune" with the Lord and each other.
   7. Team members cooperate in preparing for ministry.

III. **Ministry Phase**
   1. The supplicant feels cared for, welcomed.
   2. Team works out a plan of action with the supplicant.
   3. Supplicant feels listened to, that his/her needs are being taken seriously.
   4. Supplicant "receives" the ministry.

5. Leader sets the tone, encourages others to use their gifts, sees that all members are involved.
6. Leader keeps track of the process and helps the team to do so.
7. Team is sensitive to the supplicant and responsive to his/her needs.
8. Team is sensitive to the way the Holy Spirit is moving this session.
9. Team members support the leader.
10. All team members have a role in ministry.
11. Team members respect each other's gifts and roles in ministry.
12. Good closure with the supplicant—stopping at the right point, getting feedback from the supplicant.
13. Supplicant feels better following the ministry; was brought into the presence of Jesus.
14. Supplicant was given clear instructions about future meetings.

IV. Debriefing Phase

1. Team reviews the *process* of ministry, rather than only the content.
2. Team reviews how they functioned *as a team*.
3. Team considers what parts of the ministry were and were not effective.
4. Team reassesses the needs of the supplicant.
5. Plan is made for the next session.
6. Leader encourages each team member to reflect on his or her own gifts and *affirms* their use and development.
7. Leader helps team members to express their feelings— positive and negative—about this ministry.
8. Leader encourages the team members to continue the process of discerning their level of ministry.
9. Team leader sees whether prayer was needed by team members as a result of the ministry.
10. Leader "wraps up" the debriefing, perhaps with a prayer for the team as a whole.

Appendix B:

Checklist for Self-Reflection on Team Ministry

The following questions are useful in guiding a team's reflection upon its own ministry after one or more sessions.

1. How does the supplicant define the need for which he seeks ministry?
2. How does the team define the need for which the supplicant is seeking ministry?
3. Review briefly what the team has done in response to the supplicant's request for help.
4. What have been the results of our ministry and how successful do we judge it to have been?
5. What part of the need remains unmet? What action do we intend to take to meet the unmet need?
6. What natural skills and talent, what virtues, what charisms have been most useful in our ministry? Where does God seem to have been most present in our ministry, and where most absent?
7. It is now useful to pray for strengthening the weaknesses and deficiencies, asking God to give all that is needed to minister to this supplicant.
8. It is now proper to give praise and thanks to God for what he has done in this ministry.